D1732863

THE GLYCEMIC INDEX FOOD GUIDE CHART 2023

Your Ultimate Tool for Tracking Glycemic Load and Making Smart Food Choices

Melanie J. Lester

THE GLYCEMIC INDEX FOOD GUIDE CHART 2023

Table of Contents

Introduction: Diet To Healthy Self

Want to change your diet for better health? The Glycemic Index Food Guide Chart 2023 for Healthy Eating is a thorough reference to comprehending and applying the glycemic index for optimum health. This book is brimming with useful advice, scrumptious recipes, a list of food with their glycemic index values, and helpful tools to assist you in choosing healthier foods and enhancing your general well-being.

The glycemic index is described in terms of both what it is and how it functions. You'll discover the many kinds of carbs, how they affect blood sugar and the advantages of low-GI meals. The fundamentals of a low-GI diet are explored in further detail in the book, which also includes suggestions for portion management and advice on how to choose low-GI foods. The chart for glycemic index value for fruits, vegetables, grains, legumes, dairy products, sweeteners, processed foods, nuts, beverages, herbs, and spices is provided in detail in this book.

There are tasty low-GI dishes for breakfast, lunch, supper, and snacks. Everything from savory omelets to delicious desserts can be found here and is intended to help you maintain a healthy, balanced diet. The Glycemic Index Food Guide Chart 2023 for healthy eating is a must-read whether your goal is to manage a particular medical condition or simply enhance your general health and well-being. This book is a must-have resource for anybody trying to live a better lifestyle and enjoy life more thanks to its useful advice, delectable recipes, and helpful tools.

How To Utilize This Book As A Resource For Healthy Eating

Anybody trying to make healthy eating decisions would find the Glycemic Index Food Guide Chart 2023 to be a useful resource. The following advice will help you utilize this book effectively:

1. Understanding the Glycemic Index is essential before utilizing the guide. The book's beginning covers the fundamentals of GI and how it affects health.

2. Learn about the chart: The book includes a detailed chart of foods and their accompanying GI levels. Spend some time becoming acquainted with the chart and how to read it. Plan your meals and snacks using the chart as a guide.

3. Concentrate on low-GI foods: Including more low-GI items in your diet will help support stable

blood sugar levels and enhance general health. Use the chart to find low-GI foods and regularly incorporate them into your diet.

4. Mix meals carefully: While the GI is a helpful tool, it's crucial to keep in mind that other elements, such as fat and protein content, cooking techniques, and food pairings, can also alter glycemic reaction. When deciding how to combine various foods in your meals and snacks, use the chart as a guide.

5. Consider the book as a guide rather than a rigorous rule book: Although the Glycemic Index is a helpful tool, it's vital to keep in mind that a good diet includes many other factors as well. Make use of the book as a guide to aid in your decision-making, but don't feel obligated to strictly follow all of its advice.

6. Consult a healthcare expert: It is always a good idea to consult a healthcare practitioner if you have certain health problems or dietary requirements. They may provide you with individualized advice and assist you in incorporating the Glycemic Index into your entire dietary strategy.

Chapter 1: Glycemic Index And Your Health

How Does The Glycemic Index Work?

Those who want to better understand how various carbohydrate affects their blood sugar levels can use the Glycemic Index (GI) tool. It is a measurement of how rapidly a certain food elevates blood sugar levels after ingestion in comparison to a standard reference food, often glucose or white bread.

High GI foods are quickly absorbed and digested, which causes blood sugar levels to spike quickly. Foods with a low GI value, in comparison, take longer to digest and absorb, which causes blood sugar levels to rise more gradually. Several health advantages have been associated with eating a diet high in low GI foods, including better blood sugar regulation, better weight management, and a lower chance of developing chronic illnesses including diabetes and heart disease.

You should be aware that several variables, like the way a meal is prepared, how it was processed, when it was picked ripe, and whether or not it was consumed with other foods, can have an impact on how much GI food has.

How Does Your Health Change As A Result Of The Glycemic Index?

Your ability to manage your blood sugar, how your body responds to insulin, how much you eat, and how likely you are to develop chronic diseases like diabetes and heart disease are all influenced by your gastrointestinal system (GI). The Glycemic Index has an impact on your health, and this book will explain how to utilize it as a tool to make educated dietary decisions for your best health and wellness.

How Insulin Response And Blood Sugar Levels Connect To Each Other

The maintenance of optimal metabolic function depends on the relationship between blood sugar levels and insulin responsiveness. Your body converts the carbs you eat into glucose, which then enters your circulation and raises your blood sugar levels. The hormone insulin, which aids your cells in absorbing glucose from the bloodstream and lowering blood sugar levels, is released by your pancreas in reaction to the elevated blood sugar levels. By encouraging glucose storage for later use, insulin stimulates the liver and muscles.

The pancreas continues to secrete insulin to reduce blood sugar levels if they are persistently high, as they may be after eating high-GI meals. As a result, your body may eventually develop insulin resistance, a disease in which your cells become less receptive to insulin and you must create increasing amounts of the hormone to maintain blood sugar levels.

Obesity, type 2 diabetes, and heart disease are just a few of the health issues that insulin resistance is linked to. Blood sugar levels remain high when there is insulin resistance, which can harm the body's blood vessels, neurons, and organs. Consuming meals with low glycemic index can reduce the risk of insulin resistance and enhance blood sugar regulation. Because low-GI meals take longer to digest and absorb, their effects on blood sugar levels are more gradual. By doing so, you can support more stable blood sugar levels and avoid frequent insulin spikes.

Insulin Resistance-Related Adverse Health Effects

The metabolic disorder known as insulin resistance is marked by a decrease in the body's receptivity to the hormone insulin, which controls blood sugar levels. Increased risk for type 2 diabetes, heart disease, and other chronic health disorders are just a few of the detrimental health effects that might result from this.

The emergence of type 2 diabetes is among the major dangers connected to insulin resistance. The pancreas must create more insulin to control blood sugar levels when the body grows resistant to it, which causes the bloodstream to have persistently high levels of insulin. The pancreas's insulin-producing cells may get damaged as a result of time, which may decrease the amount of insulin produced and cause blood sugar levels to rise even higher. In the long run, type 2 diabetes may develop as a result of this vicious cycle.

Moreover, a higher risk of heart disease is linked to insulin resistance. The formation of atherosclerosis, or the accumulation of plaque in the arteries, can be brought on by high insulin levels in the circulation damaging blood vessels. This might make cardiovascular events like heart attacks, strokes, and other problems more likely. Insulin resistance has been associated with several unfavorable health outcomes, including polycystic ovarian syndrome (PCOS), fatty liver disease, and several forms of cancer, in addition to its detrimental impact on blood sugar and cardiovascular health.

Thankfully, lifestyle adjustments including altered eating habits, consistent exercise, and weight control may frequently prevent or reverse insulin resistance. In addition to enhancing insulin sensitivity, adopting a diet low in refined carbs and high in fiber, protein, and healthy fats helps lower the chance of developing insulin resistance and its related health issues.

The Glycemic Index's Possible Drawbacks And Issues As A Dietary Tool

Even though the Glycemic Index (GI) can be a valuable tool for controlling blood sugar levels and encouraging weight reduction, there may be drawbacks and disagreements about its application as a dietary tool.

One drawback of the GI is that it only takes into account how carbs affect blood sugar levels; it ignores other aspects of food, such as fat and protein content, cooking techniques, and meal pairings, which can also have an impact on how the body reacts to carbohydrates. As an illustration, adding fat or protein to a dish with a high GI can aid in decreasing the glycemic response by slowing down the digestion and absorption of carbs. As a result, relying exclusively on the GI to inform dietary decisions would not always give a clear picture of how various meals can alter blood sugar levels.

The GI's potential for considerable individual variation based on elements including heredity, age, and amount of physical activity is yet another drawback. So, it may not always be possible to generalize advice for everyone because the GI of a given item may vary across all individuals.

The use of the GI as a nutritional aid is likewise controversial. The complicated nature of nutrition and dietary options, according to some critics, maybe oversimplified by this method, and it may not be a useful tool for everyone. For some, concentrating on overall calorie intake and portion management rather than a particular glycemic response, for instance, maybe more beneficial.

Furthermore, if only low-GI meals are consumed, some experts worry that this may limit dietary diversity and even result in vitamin deficits if specific items are left out. It is crucial to remember that other recognized dietary recommendations should be utilized in addition to, not as a substitute for, the GI.

Chapter 2: Glycemic Index And Carbohydrates: Understanding The Connection

The Function Of Carbs In Your Diet

Being the major source of energy for our body and brain cells, carbohydrates are crucial for sustaining peak health and well-being. Carbon, hydrogen, and oxygen are the three components that makeup carbohydrates. They are divided into two primary groups: simple carbs and complicated carbohydrates. Simple carbs may be found in foods like fruits, milk, and candies and are composed of just one or two sugar molecules. Contrarily, complex carbohydrates are found in foods like whole grains, vegetables, and legumes and are made up of lengthy chains of sugar molecules.

To keep blood sugar levels steady, carbohydrates are essential. When we ingest carbs, they are converted to glucose and absorbed into our circulation. Next, as a means of aiding the uptake of glucose by our cells, our body creates insulin, a hormone that aids in controlling blood sugar levels. Moreover, insulin aids in the storage of extra glucose as glycogen in our muscles and liver.

Moreover, carbohydrates encourage physical activity and exercise. During the activity, glucose serves as the main fuel source for our muscles. Maintaining energy levels and endurance during physical exercise depends on consuming enough carbohydrates.

Choosing nutritious sources and consuming carbs in moderation is crucial for preserving good health. A diet rich in simple carbohydrates, such as sugar and refined grains, can cause weight gain, insulin resistance, and a higher chance of developing chronic illnesses including type 2 diabetes and heart disease. Selecting complex carbs from whole foods like fruits, vegetables, and whole grains may offer a variety of nutrients and enhance general health and well-being.

How The Body Uses Carbs

The body uses carbohydrates as a significant source of energy and they are essential for preserving good health. When we eat carbs, the body converts them into simple sugars like glucose, which may be utilized as fuel by our cells. Salivary enzymes start to break down complex carbs into simpler sugars in the mouth, where the process of digesting carbohydrates starts.

While in the stomach, stomach acid and digestive enzymes continue to break down these carbs. From there, the carbs enter the small intestine, where pancreatic and intestinal enzymes finish the digestive process by converting the remaining complex carbohydrates to simple sugars.

After the carbs have been converted to simple sugars, they are absorbed into circulation and delivered to the liver. By releasing glucose into the circulation when levels are low and storing extra glucose as glycogen for later use, the liver helps to control blood sugar levels. Blood sugar levels are significantly regulated by the hormone insulin, which is generated by the pancreas. After a meal, as blood sugar levels rise, insulin is produced to assist in the transportation of glucose from the bloodstream into our cells for energy. Moreover, insulin aids in the storage of extra glucose as glycogen in the muscles and liver.

Unused carbohydrates are eventually turned into fat and kept in adipose tissue. This is why ingesting too many carbs, especially simple carbohydrates like sugar and refined grains, can result in weight gain and obesity. To promote optimum health and well-being, it is crucial to pick nutritious carbs from whole food sources including fruits, vegetables, and whole grains. These carbs frequently contain a lot of fiber and other necessary elements that help with metabolism, digestion, and general health.

Analysis Of The Glycemic Index

The pace at which carbohydrates in meals increase blood sugar levels after ingestion is gauged by the Glycemic Index (GI), a rating system. The GI is based on a scale from 0 to 100, with higher values suggesting a quicker rise in blood sugar levels. Meals with a high GI score are quickly digested and absorbed, which causes a jump in blood sugar levels, whereas foods with a low GI score are digested and absorbed more slowly, which causes a longer increase in blood sugar levels.

The blood sugar response of a group of people to a fixed amount of carbohydrates in a certain food is measured to determine the GI. The blood sugar reaction is then compared to the response to the same quantity of carbohydrates in a reference meal, often pure glucose or white bread. The resultant value is the food's GI score.

Understanding how to interpret the GI score will help you manage your blood sugar levels and make nutritious meal selections. Meals with a low GI score (55 or less) are seen as healthier alternatives because they cause a more gradual rise in blood sugar levels, which helps to maintain consistent energy levels and prevents insulin spikes. Fruits, vegetables, whole grains, legumes, and nuts are a few of these foods. Foods with a high GI score (70 or more) should only be eaten seldom since they can quickly elevate blood sugar levels, which can result in insulin resistance, weight gain, and other health problems. White bread, sweetened beverages, confections, and processed snacks are some of these items.

It is significant to remember that there are other factors to take into account while selecting nutritious foods in addition to GI. Together with other macro-nutrients, fiber, and micro-nutrients, the kind and amount of carbs should also be considered. The greatest method to guarantee optimum health and well-being is to eat a balanced diet that includes a range of whole foods.

Variables That Influence A Food's Glycemic Index

A food's Glycemic Index (GI) is impacted by several additional elements in addition to the type of carbohydrates it contains. These are several elements that may have an impact on a food's GI:

1. Fruits and vegetables alter in terms of their carbohydrate content as they mature, which can have an impact on their GI. Ripe bananas, for instance, have a higher GI than unripe bananas.

2. Processing and cooking techniques: Processing and cooking techniques can change the structure

of carbs, which can impact the GI. This can make them easier or harder to digest. For instance, cooking pasta until it is al dente (hard) as opposed to soft leads to a lower GI.

3. Fiber Content: Fiber reduces the pace at which carbs are absorbed in the digestive tract and so lowers a food's GI. Compared to processed meals, whole grains, fruits, and vegetables are often richer in fiber and have a lower GI.

4. Content of fat and protein: Consuming meals high in fat and protein with carbs might delay their absorption and digestion, lowering the meal's glycemic index (GI).

5. Combinations of foods: The total GI of a meal can be impacted by pairing high-GI items with low-GI foods. A meal's overall GI can be lowered, for instance, by combining a high GI dish like white rice with a low GI food like vegetables.

6. Diversity of cultivars and species: Due to their differing compositions, various varieties of the same food might have different GI ratings.

It is essential to remember that GI is not a precise science and might vary based on several circumstances. However, being aware of these elements might aid in making wise choices when it comes to preparing meals and choosing foods.

Chapter 3: Making The Best Food Selections For A Low-GI Diet

A growing number of people are turning to low-GI eating as a healthy eating strategy that can help with blood sugar control, lower the chance of developing chronic illnesses like diabetes, heart disease, and obesity, and enhance general health and well-being. When you first start eating low-GI, it could feel daunting. Yet with some basic information and preparation, it's simple to adopt this strategy into your diet and take advantage of the many health advantages it offers.

Low-GI diet can help beginners control their blood sugar levels, increase their energy levels, and keep a healthy weight. Little dietary adjustments, like switching from white to whole-grain bread, can have a significant impact on your health and well-being. Beginners may make educated food decisions that are good for their health and prevent chronic illnesses by learning the fundamentals of low-GI eating.

Low-GI Eating Basics For Beginners

Here are some tips to help you get started if you want to include low-GI (Glycemic Index) items in your diet:

1. Choose entire, unprocessed foods: As they often have a lower GI than processed foods, choose whole foods including fruits, vegetables, whole grains, legumes, nuts, and nuts in their original condition.

2. Concentrate on fiber: Foods with a high fiber content, such as whole grains, vegetables, and legumes, typically have a lower GI. These meals can stabilize blood sugar levels and prolong your sensation of fullness.

3. Mix with protein and healthy fats: You may decrease your meals' overall GI by including protein and healthy fats in your meals. For your meals, think about incorporating almonds, avocados, or lean protein sources.

4. Avoid highly processed meals: White bread, white rice, and sugary snacks are examples of processed foods that tend to have a higher GI. Use whole-grain varieties of bread and pasta instead, and go for fruits rather than sugary treats.

5. Choosing low-GI fruits is a good idea since some fruits, including apples, berries, and grapefruit, have a lower GI than others. Try to include some of these in your meals and snacks.

6. Foods with high and low GI should be combined in a meal to maintain a healthy GI level. For instance, combine veggies or lean protein with white rice, a dish with a high glycemic index.

7. Look at the label: On the label of many packaged goods, the GI is indicated. When adding a food item to your cart, make sure you check its GI rating.

8. Think ahead: Plan out your meals and snacks using the GI chart. This might help you make sure your diet contains an adequate amount of low-GI items.

9. Try out new meals: There are a ton of delectable low-GI recipes online. See which ones work best for you and your family by experimenting with a few.

10. Keep in mind that portion sizes matter since even low-GI meals can produce blood sugar increases if ingested in big amounts. Consider including low-GI snacks throughout the day and be cautious of your portion sizes to help control your blood sugar levels.

How To Understand And Read Nutrition Labels

Meals with a low GI rating are broken down more slowly and result in a gradual rise in blood sugar levels, foods with a high GI rating are broken down fast and cause a rapid surge in blood sugar levels. You can control your blood sugar levels and enhance your general health by selecting meals with a lower GI rating. When purchasing low-GI foods, it is important to understand how to read and interpret nutrition labels.

Advice on How to Read and Understand Nutrition Labels:

i. Start with the serving size: You can get a better understanding of how much food you should be consuming by looking at the serving size on the label. To be sure you are comparing like servings, pay attention to this.

ii. Check the label for the total amount of carbs: this includes both simple and complex carbohydrates. This figure will give you a basic indication of the food's carb content.

iii. Scan for fiber: A lower GI is typically associated with high-fiber diets, therefore seek out these items.

The amount of fiber should appear after the overall amount of carbs.

iv. Determine the net carbs: Certain low-GI diets emphasize the net carbs, which are determined by deducting the fiber from the total amount of carbohydrates. This might help you determine the precise number of carbs that will affect your blood sugar levels.

v. Be mindful of added sugars: since they might induce blood sugar spikes, so it's crucial to restrict your consumption. Be on the lookout for meals with minimal to no added sugar.

vi. Examine the amount of fat: While historically low-fat diets have been quite popular, research has revealed that good fats can help regulate blood sugar levels. Seek meals that are high in healthy fats, such as almonds and avocados.

vii. Check out the ingredient list: Your understanding of the food's quality will be improved by reading the ingredients list. As much as you can, try to get entire, unprocessed foods.

viii. Compare several brands: To select the greatest low-GI food alternative, it's vital to evaluate various brands and products. Compare the nutritional content of various brands and look for items with a low GI rating.

ix. Fresh vegetables, healthy grains, and unprocessed goods are typically found outside of the grocery store, so shop there. To find low-GI foods, concentrate your shopping in this region.

x. Prepare your meals in advance to help you stay on track with a balanced diet and steer clear of high glycemic index items. Search for low-GI dishes and structure your meals around them.

xi. You can choose wisely when you shop for low-GI meals by adhering to these suggestions. Pay attention to the nutritious composition of various items and emphasize complete, unprocessed meals.

A Guide To Low-GI Cooking And Meal Preparation

Planning and preparing low-GI meals, however, might be difficult, especially if you're used to a diet heavy in refined carbs. The good news is that you can increase the amount of low-GI items in your diet by following a variety of easy cooking and meal prep strategies.

1. Emphasizing whole, unprocessed foods is the simplest approach to make sure you're consuming low-GI meals. Processed foods have a higher GI than these items, which include fruits, vegetables, lean protein, and whole grains.

2. Employ healthy cooking techniques: A food's GI can be affected by the cooking process. In comparison to baking or roasting, boiling potatoes have a higher GI. To reduce the GI of your food, choose healthy cooking techniques including grilling, baking, and sautéing.

3. Increase the amount of fiber in your diet: Foods with a high fiber content, such as fruits, vegetables, legumes, whole grains, and cereals, have a lower GI because fiber slows down the absorption of glucose into the circulation. To increase meal fullness and minimize GI, include fiber-rich foods in your diet.

4. Choose grains with a low GI: Instead of white rice or pasta, choose grains with a lower GI, such as quinoa, barley, and brown rice.

5. Utilize low-GI sweeteners: Stevia, monk fruit, and other low-GI alternatives to sugar and

high-fructose corn syrup can be used to sweeten meals and beverages.

6. Add good fats to your diet: Doing so can reduce your meal's GI and increase its filling power. Examples of healthy fats to include in your diet are avocado, almonds, and olive oil.

7. Prepare your meals in advance: Making healthier choices throughout the week can be facilitated by planning and preparing your meals. For usage in several meals throughout the week, prepare big quantities of low-GI items like quinoa or roasted vegetables.

8. Use spices and herbs to add taste to your food without adding extra calories or raising the GI by experimenting with different combinations. You may improve the flavor of your low-GI meals by adding herbs and spices like cinnamon and turmeric and flavors like basil or rosemary.

9. Be mindful of your portion sizes because even low-GI meals can contain a lot of calories if you eat them in excess. By using smaller dishes, weighing your food, and paying attention to serving sizes, you may practice portion management.

10. See a qualified dietitian for advice: A dietician can assist you in creating low-GI meals that suit your dietary requirements and tastes. They can also provide you with advice on how to sustainably adopt a low-GI diet into your way of life.

Chapter 4: Your Comprehensive Glycemic Index Food Guide

List Of Everyday Foods And Their Glycemic Index Scores

Anybody wishing to follow a low glycemic index diet would benefit from having a thorough list of common foods and their Glycemic Index values. How rapidly carbohydrates in a diet boost blood sugar levels are determined by the Glycemic Index (GI). One can lessen the chance of developing chronic diseases like diabetes and heart disease by eating foods with a lower GI.

This can also assist to control blood sugar levels and encourage weight reduction. People can choose what they eat wisely and understand how it affects their bodies by having access to a complete list of common foods and their GI values.

The information in this list covers dairy items, sweeteners, processed foods, nuts, beverages, herbs, and spices in addition to fruits, vegetables, grains, legumes, dairy products, and sweeteners. Plan your meals more effectively and follow this guide to healthy eating by knowing the GI levels of various foods.

Fruits And Their GI Values

	Fruit	Weight	GI Value
1.	Honeydew melon	100g	65
2.	Pineapple	100g	66
3.	Papaya	140g	68
4.	Mango	120g	69
5.	Apricot	35g	69
6.	Watermelon	100g	72
7.	Dates	50g	72
8.	Figs	50g	74
9.	Grapes	80g	75
10.	Raisins	50g	76
11.	Cherries	100g	77
12.	Pomegranate	100g	77
13.	Kiwi	70g	79
14.	Banana	120g	79
15.	Peach	100g	79
16.	Tangerine	100g	80
17.	Apple	120g	81
18.	Nectarine	120g	81
19.	Orange	140g	83
20.	Persimmon	100g	83
21.	Grapefruit	123g	83
22.	Plum	65g	85
23.	Cantaloupe	100g	85
24.	Blueberries	100g	85
25.	Pineapple juice	240ml	86
26.	Mango juice	240ml	88

Fruit	Weight	GI Value
27. Guava	55g	89
28. Fruit cocktail	100g	90
29. Passion fruit	18g	93
30. Cranberry juice	240ml	94
31. Prunes	50g	95
32. Raisin bran cereal	30g	98
33. Raisin bread	30g	98
34. Dried apricots	35g	101
35. Raisin bran muffin	60g	103
36. Dried dates	50g	103
37. Fig bars	30g	104
38. Fruit roll-up	30g	99
39. Lemonade	240ml	103
40. Banana bread	60g	105
41. Pop tarts	50g	114
42. Jelly beans	40g	80-115
43. Dried cranberries	40g	114
44. Honey	21g	55-83
45. Pina colada	240ml	106
46. Canned fruit cocktail	100g	94-108
47. Blueberry muffin	60g	113
48. Fruit snacks	20g	99-118
49. Orange juice with pulp	240ml	109
50. Glazed donut	60g	108
51. Caramel apple	100g	109
52. Banana chips	14g	51-110
53. Grape juice	240ml	111

Fruit	Weight	GI Value
54. Blueberry pie	80g	114
55. Strawberry jam	20g	51-115
56. Apple, raw, with skin	120g	36
57. Apricot, raw	35g	57
58. Avocado, raw	30g	15
59. Banana, ripe	118g	51
60. Berries, mixed, unsweetened (120 g)		40
61. Blackberry, raw	144g	25
62. Blueberries, raw	148g	53
63. Cantaloupe, raw	177g	65
64. Carambola, raw	91g	31
65. Cherry, raw	85g	22
66. Clementine, raw	74g	35
67. Coconut, raw	80g	45
68. Cranberries, unsweetened, raw (110 g)		45
69. Date, medjool	24g	53
70. Dragon fruit, raw	198g	60
71. Durian, raw	243g	44
72. Elderberries, raw	145g	79
73. Fig, raw	50g	61
74. Gooseberries, raw	150g	34
75. Grapefruit, raw	123g	25
76. Grapes, raw	92g	46
77. Guava, raw	55g	12
78. Honeydew melon, raw (177 g)		64
79. Jackfruit, raw	151g	48
80. Jujube, raw	28g	50

Fruit	Weight	GI Value
81. Kiwi, raw	69g	53
82. Kumquat, raw	19g	6
83. Lemon, raw	58g	20
84. Lime, raw	67g	24
85. Longan, raw	20g	58
86. Lychee, raw	10g	57
87. Mango, raw	165g	51
88. Mandarin orange, raw (88 g)		42
89. Mulberry, raw	140g	25
90. Nectarine, raw	136g	43
91. Orange, raw	131g	42
92. Papaya, raw	140g	58
93. Passion fruit, raw	18g	30
94. Peach, raw	150g	42
95. Pear, raw	166g	38
96. Persimmon, raw	168g	71
97. Pineapple, raw	165g	59
98. Plum, raw	65g	39
99. Pomegranate, raw	87g	53
100. Pomelo, raw	(244 g)	32

Vegetables And Their GI Values

Vegetable	Weight	GI Value
1. Arugula	100g	20
2. Asparagus, boiled	100g	15

	Vegetable	Weight	GI Value
3.	Bamboo shoots, boiled (100g)		20
4.	Beet greens	100g	15
5.	Beets, boiled	100g	64
6.	Bell peppers, green, raw (100g)		10
7.	Bell peppers, red, raw	100g	10
8.	Bitter gourd, cooked	100g	15
9.	Bok choy, cooked	100g	10
10.	Broccoli, boiled	100g	10
11.	Brussels sprouts, boiled (100g)		10
12.	Cabbage, green, boiled	100g	10
13.	Cabbage, red, boiled	100g	10
14.	Carrots, boiled	100g	39
15.	Cauliflower, boiled	100g	10
16.	Celery, raw	100g	15
17.	Chard, Swiss, boiled	100g	10
18.	Chicory greens	100g	15
19.	Chinese cabbage, boiled (100g)		10
20.	Collard greens, boiled (100g)		10
21.	Cucumber, peeled, raw	100g	15
22.	Eggplant, boiled	100g	10
23.	Endive, raw	100g	15
24.	Fennel, boiled	100g	15
25.	Garlic, raw	100g	15
26.	Ginger root, raw	100g	15
27.	Green beans, boiled	100g	15
28.	Jicama, boiled	100g	50
29.	Kale, boiled	100g	10

	Vegetable	Weight	GI Value
30.	Kohlrabi, boiled	100g	15
31.	Leeks, boiled	100g	10
32.	Lettuce, green leaf, raw	100g	10
33.	Lettuce, iceberg, raw	100g	10
34.	Lettuce, red leaf, raw	100g	10
35.	Lima beans, boiled	100g	30
36.	Mushrooms, boiled	100g	10
37.	Mustard greens, boiled	100g	10
38.	Okra, boiled	100g	20
39.	Onion, boiled	100g	10
40.	Parsley, raw	100g	5
41.	Parsnips, boiled	100g	50
42.	Peas, boiled	100g	40
43.	Peppers, hot chili, raw	100g	10
44.	Peppers, sweet, raw	100g	10
45.	Potatoes, boiled, with skin (100g)		56
46.	Pumpkin, boiled	100g	75
47.	Radicchio, raw	100g	15
48.	Radish, raw	100g	15
49.	Rhubarb, boiled	100g	15
50.	Rutabaga, boiled	100g	50
51.	Scallions, raw	100g	10
52.	Shallots, boiled	100g	10
53.	Snow peas, boiled	100g	50
54.	Sorrel, raw	100g	10
55.	Soybeans, boiled	100g	15
56.	Spinach, boiled	100g	10

	Vegetable	Weight	GI Value
57.	Squash, summer, boiled (100g)		15
58.	Squash, winter, boiled 100g		50
59.	Sweet potato, boiled	100g	54
60.	Swiss chard, boiled	100g	10
61.	Tomatillos, raw	100g	10
62.	Tomatoes, raw	100g	15
63.	Turnips, boiled	100g	55
64.	Watercress, raw	100g	10
65.	Wax beans, boiled	100g	15
66.	Zucchini, boiled	100g	15
67.	Acorn squash, baked	100g	75
68.	Alfalfa sprouts, raw	100g	5
69.	Amaranth leaves, boiled	100g	35
70.	Arrowroot, boiled	100g	70
71.	Beetroot, raw	100g	61
72.	Brussels sprouts, frozen, boiled (100g)		40
73.	Butternut squash, baked	100g	75
74.	Carrots, raw	100g	47
75.	Cassava, boiled	100g	46
76.	Cauliflower, raw	100g	5
77.	Chayote, boiled	100g	35
78.	Chicory greens, raw	100g	5
79.	Corn, boiled	100g	55
80.	Dandelion greens, raw	100g	5
81.	Edamame, boiled	100g	30
82.	Eggplant, boiled	100g	10
83.	Endive, raw	100g	15

84.	Fennel, raw	100g	15
85.	Ginger root, raw	100g	0
	Vegetable	Weight	GI Value
86.	Green beans, boiled	100g	15
87.	Jerusalem artichoke, raw (100g)		50
88.	Jicama, raw	100g	50
89.	Kale, boiled	100g	5
90.	Kohlrabi, boiled	100g	50
91.	Leeks, boiled	100g	15
92.	Lentils, boiled	100g	30
93.	Lettuce, butterhead, raw (100g)		15
94.	Lettuce, cos, raw	100g	15
95.	Lettuce, green leaf, raw	100g	10
96.	Lettuce, iceberg, raw	100g	10
97.	Lettuce, red leaf, raw	100g	10
98.	Lima beans, boiled	100g	30

Grains And Their GI Values

	Grains	Weight	GI Value
1)	Rice (white)	150g	73
2)	Barley	100g	22
3)	Oatmeal (rolled)	100g	55
4)	Bulgur	100g	48
5)	Quinoa	100g	53
6)	Couscous	100g	65
7)	Buckwheat	100g	54

		Weight	GI Value
8)	Spelt	100g	54
9)	Farro	100g	45
10)	Cornmeal	100g	68
11)	Amaranth	100g	65
	Grains	Weight	GI Value
12)	Wheat berries	100g	41
13)	Millet	100g	71
14)	Rye berries	100g	41
15)	Sorghum	100g	70
16)	Kamut	100g	45
17)	Teff	100g	74
18)	Freekeh	100g	43
19)	Fonio	100g	85
20)	Spelt flakes	100g	46
21)	Whole wheat flour	100g	74
22)	Buckwheat flour	100g	71
23)	Rye flour	100g	41
24)	Triticale flour	100g	55
25)	Barley flour	100g	36
26)	Corn flour	100g	68
27)	Spelt flour	100g	54
28)	Kamut flour	100g	45
29)	Oat bran	100g	55
30)	Wheat bran	100g	51
31)	Bulgur (cooked)	150g	46
32)	Quinoa (cooked)	150g	53
33)	Couscous (cooked)	150g	65
34)	Brown rice	150g	68

	Grains	Weight	GI Value
35)	White rice (parboiled) (150g)		38
36)	White rice (instant)	150g	87
37)	Wild rice	150g	57
38)	Oatmeal (instant)	40g	83
39)	Cream of wheat	100g	70
40)	Farina	100g	66
41)	Rice cakes (brown)	20g	82
42)	Rice cakes (white)	20g	77
43)	Corn tortillas	50g	52
44)	Whole wheat tortillas (50g)		30
45)	Cornbread	100g	68
46)	Oatcakes	40g	55
47)	Wheat crackers	20g	74
48)	Brown rice crackers	20g	82
49)	White bread	50g	70
50)	Whole wheat bread	50g	69
51)	Corn flakes	30g	93
52)	Puffed rice cereal	30g	82
53)	Quinoa (cooked)	100g	53
54)	Couscous (cooked)	100g	65
55)	Bulgur (cooked)	100g	46
56)	Millet (cooked)	100g	71
57)	Barley (cooked)	100g	28
58)	Oat bran cereal	30g	55
59)	Steel-cut oats (cooked) (100g)		42
60)	Rolled oats (cooked)	(100g)	55
61)	Instant oats (cooked)	(100g)	83

	Weight	GI Value
62) Brown rice (cooked)	(100g)	50
63) White rice (cooked)	(100g)	73
64) Wild rice (cooked)	(100g)	57
65) Buckwheat groats (cooked)	(100g)	54
Grains	Weight	GI Value
66) Farro (cooked)	100g	45
67) Freekeh (cooked)	100g	43
68) Amaranth (cooked)	100g	65
69) Kamut (cooked)	100g	45
70) Spelt (cooked)	100g	54
71) Triticale (cooked)	100g	58
72) Teff (cooked)	100g	74
73) Fonio (cooked)	100g	58
74) Job's tears (cooked)	100g	72
75) Sorghum (cooked)	100g	62
76) Wheat berries (cooked)	100g	30
77) Popcorn (air-popped)	30g	65
78) Rice cakes	20g	82
79) Corn tortillas	50g	52
80) Wheat tortillas	50g	52
81) Whole wheat bread	50g	74
82) White bread	50g	75
83) Sourdough bread	50g	53
84) Baguette (white)	50g	95
85) Baguette (whole wheat)	50g	96
86) Rye crispbread	20g	64
87) Rice crackers	20g	87
88) Wheat crackers	20g	74

	Grains	Weight	GI Value
89)	Popcorn cakes	20g	70
90)	Whole wheat pita bread	50g	57
91)	White pita bread	50g	68
92)	Whole wheat English muffin (50g)		45
	Grains	Weight	GI Value
93)	White English muffin	50g	77
94)	Brown rice cakes	20g	82
95)	White rice cakes	20g	78
96)	Buckwheat soba noodles (cooked)	100g	46
97)	Barley flakes cereal	30g	66
98)	Quinoa flakes cereal	30g	78
99)	Buckwheat flour	100g	54
100)	Oat flour	100g	55

Legumes And Their GI Values

	Legumes	Weight	GI Value
1.	Adzuki beans	20-40g	19-32
2.	Black beans	25-50g	20-30
3.	Black-eyed peas	20-40g	33-46
4.	Borlotti beans	25-50g	20-30
5.	Broad beans	30-60g	31-45
6.	Butter beans	30-60g	31-45
7.	Cannellini beans	25-50g	31-45
8.	Chickpeas	20-40g	28-36
9.	Cowpeas	20-40g	28-40

	Legumes	Weight	GI Value
10.	Fava beans	30-60g	26-36
11.	Flageolet beans	20-40g	40-50
12.	Garbanzo beans	20-40g	28-36
13.	Great Northern beans	25-50g	31-45
14.	Kidney beans	25-50g	20-30
15.	Lentils	20-40g	20-30
	Legumes	Weight	GI Value
16.	Lima beans	30-60g	32-44
17.	Lupin beans	20-40g	31-45
18.	Mung beans	20-40g	25-45
19.	Navy beans	25-50g	31-45
20.	Peanuts	15-30g	13-15
21.	Pigeon peas	20-40g	25-35
22.	Pink beans	25-50g	20-30
23.	Pinto beans	25-50g	20-30
24.	Red lentils	20-40g	25-30
25.	Soybeans	20-40g	15-20
26.	Split peas	20-40g	22-28
27.	White beans	25-50g	31-45
28.	Yellow split peas	20-40g	22-28
29.	Alfalfa sprouts	50-100g	15-20
30.	Bean sprouts	50-100g	30-40
31.	Broccoli sprouts	50-100g	15-20
32.	Buckwheat sprouts	50-100g	30-40
33.	Cabbage sprouts	50-100g	30-40
34.	Chickpea sprouts	50-100g	30-40
35.	Green lentil sprouts	50-100g	30-40
36.	Green lentil sprouts	50-100g	30-40

		Weight	GI Value
37.	Kidney bean sprouts	50-100g	30-40
38.	Lentil sprouts	50-100g	30-40
39.	Mung bean sprouts	50-100g	25-45
40.	Pea sprouts	50-100g	30-40
41.	Soybean sprouts	50-100g	15-20
42.	Winged bean sprouts	50-100g	20-30
	Legumes	Weight	GI Value
43.	Winged beans	25-50g	25-35
44.	Azuki bean sprouts	50-100g	20-30
45.	Black bean sprouts	50-100g	20-30
46.	Broad bean sprouts	50-100g	31-45
47.	Chickpea flour	20-40g	40-50
48.	Cowpea flour	20-40g	30-40
49.	Fava bean flour	20-40g	26-36
50.	Green lentil flour	20-40g	20-30
51.	Kidney bean flour	20-40g	20-30
52.	Mung bean flour	20-40g	25-45
53.	Pea flour	20-40g	30-40
54.	Pinto bean flour	20-40g	20-30
55.	Soy flour	20-40g	15-20
56.	White bean flour	20-40g	31-45
57.	Chickpea noodles	50-100g	35-45
58.	Green lentil noodles	50-100g	20-30
59.	Mung bean noodles	50-100g	25-45
60.	Pea noodles	50-100g	30-40
61.	Soybean noodles	50-100g	15-20
62.	Adzuki bean noodles	50-100g	19-32
63.	Black bean noodles	50-100g	20-30

64.	Chickpea pasta	50-100g	35-45
65.	Green lentil pasta	50-100g	20-30
66.	Mung bean pasta	50-100g	25-45
67.	Pea pasta	50-100g	30-40
68.	Soybean pasta	50-100g	15-20
69.	Adzuki bean pasta	50-100g	19-32
	Legumes	Weight	GI Value
70.	Cannellini beans	50-100g	31-45
71.	Garbanzo beans	50-100g	28-36
72.	Lima beans	50-100g	20-30
73.	Moth beans	50-100g	30-40
74.	Navy beans	50-100g	30-40
75.	Pink beans	50-100g	31-45
76.	Small red beans	50-100g	31-45
77.	Cranberry beans	50-100g	31-45
78.	Turtle beans	50-100g	20-30
79.	Winged beans	25-50g	25-35
80.	Pinto beans	50-100g	31-45
81.	French beans	50-100g	15-20
82.	Black-eyed peas	50-100g	31-45
83.	Snow peas	50-100g	15-20
84.	Sugar snap peas	50-100g	15-20
85.	Cowpeas	50-100g	25-35
86.	Hyacinth beans	50-100g	25-35
87.	Moong dal	20-40g	25-35
88.	Toor dal	20-40g	35-45
89.	Chana dal	20-40g	30-40
90.	Urad dal	20-40g	25-35

	Legumes	Weight	GI Value
91.	Masoor dal	20-40g	30-40
92.	Yellow split peas	20-40g	32-45
93.	Green split peas	20-40g	25-35
94.	Chickpea hummus	20-40g	6-16
95.	Black bean hummus	20-40g	15-25
96.	Edamame	50-100g	18-30
	Legumes	Weight	GI Value
97.	Chickpea falafel	20-40g	50-60
98.	Black bean burgers	50-100g	20-30
99.	Lentil soup	240g	44
100.	Split pea soup	240g	48
101.	Re-fried beans	100-150g	36-40

The GI Values Of Dairy Products

Please be aware that based on the individual brand or category of goods, weight, and GI values might change.

	Dairy Products	Volume	GI Value
1)	Milk (whole)	250 mL	41
2)	Milk (2%)	250 mL	41
3)	Milk (1%)	250 mL	32
4)	Milk (skim)	250 mL	32
5)	Almond milk (unsweetened)	250 mL	25
6)	Soy milk (unsweetened)	250 mL	31
7)	Chocolate milk (whole)	250 mL	65
8)	Chocolate milk (2%)	250 mL	65

	Dairy Products	Volume/Weight	GI Value
9)	Chocolate milk (1%)	250 mL	52
10)	Chocolate milk (skim)	250 mL	52
11)	Buttermilk	250 mL	34
12)	Cream (whipping)	15 mL	0
13)	Cream (heavy)	15 mL	0
14)	Cream (light)	15 mL	0
15)	Cream (sour)	15 mL	0
16)	Yogurt (plain)	125 mL	14
17)	Yogurt (low-fat, plain)	125 mL	33
18)	Yogurt (fruit)	125 mL	41
19)	Greek yogurt (plain)	125 mL	11
20)	Greek yogurt (low-fat, plain)	125 mL	28
21)	Greek yogurt (fruit)	125 mL	47
22)	Cheese (cheddar)	30 g	0
23)	Cheese (mozzarella)	30 g	0
24)	Cheese (Swiss)	30 g	0
25)	Cheese (goat)	30 g	0
26)	Cheese (brie)	30 g	0
27)	Cottage cheese (2%)	125 mL	10
28)	Cottage cheese (1%)	125 mL	10
29)	Cottage cheese (low-fat)	125 mL	10
30)	Ricotta cheese (part-skim)	125 mL	35
31)	Feta cheese	30 g	0
32)	Cream cheese	15 g	0
33)	Butter	15g	0
34)	Margarine	15 g	0
35)	Ice cream (vanilla)	125 mL	61

	Volume/Weight	GI Value
36) Ice cream (chocolate)	125 mL	70
37) Ice cream (strawberry)	125 mL	62
38) Sorbet (lemon)	125 mL	50
39) Sorbet (raspberry)	125 mL	48
40) Whipped cream	15 mL	0
41) Eggnog	250 mL	84
42) Half and half	15 mL	0
43) Condensed milk	15 mL	61
Dairy Products	Volume/Weight	GI Value
44) Evaporated milk	15 mL	27
45) Powdered milk	15 g	31
46) Chocolate cheese spread	15 g	50
47) Cheesecake (1 slice)	80 g	38
48) Pudding (vanilla)	125 mL	45
49) Pudding (chocolate)	125 mL	51
50) Pudding (butterscotch)	125 mL	48
51) Milkshake (vanilla)	250 mL	67
52) Milkshake (chocolate)	250 mL	68
53) Milkshake (strawberry)	250 mL	66
54) Creamed spinach	125 g	7
55) Creamed corn	125 g	52
56) Sour cream	15 mL	0
57) Cheese sauce	15 mL	70
58) Alfredo sauce	15 mL	45
59) Tzatziki	15 mL	7
60) Clotted cream	15 mL	0
61) Custard	125 mL	46
62) Flan	125 g	42

63) Milk chocolate	30 g	49
64) Dark chocolate	30 g	23
65) White chocolate	30 g	43
66) Hot chocolate	250 mL	49
67) Caramel sauce	15 mL	40
68) Dulce de leche	15 g	60
69) Butterscotch sauce	15 mL	60
70) Creme brulee	125 g	46

Dairy Products	Volume/Weight	GI Value
71) Rice pudding	125 mL	63
72) Bread pudding	125 g	54
73) Macaroni and cheese	125 g	64
74) Cheeseburger	1	33
75) Pizza	1 slice	80
76) Quesadilla	1	50
77) Nachos with cheese	125 g	42
78) Cheesy garlic bread	1 slice	38
79) Croissant with cheese	1	67
80) Grilled cheese sandwich	1	39
81) Cheese and crackers (30 g cheese, 5 crackers)		28
82) Cheese fondue	125 mL	30
83) Cheese souffle	125 g	35
84) Cheese omelette	1	32
85) Scrambled eggs with cheese	125 g	32
86) Quiche	125 g	39
87) Frittata	125 g	33
88) Cream of mushroom soup	250 mL	55
89) Cream of broccoli soup	250 mL	54

	Volume/Weight	GI Value
90) Cream of tomato soup	250 mL	38
91) Cream of chicken soup	250 mL	50
92) Cream of asparagus soup	250 mL	37
93) Cream of celery soup	250 mL	52
94) Cream of potato soup	250 mL	51
95) Cream of corn soup	250 mL	56
96) Cream of shrimp soup	250 mL	55
97) Cream of spinach soup	250 mL	45
Dairy Products	Volume/Weight	GI Value
98) Cream of cauliflower soup	250 mL	47
99) Cream of leek soup	250 mL	35
100) Cream of beet soup	250 mL	64

Note: GI values may vary depending on the brand and specific recipe used for each product.

Sweeteners And Their GI Values

Sweeteners	Weight	GI Value
1. Agave nectar	1 tsp (5g)	30-40
2. Aspartame	1 packet (0.5g)	0
3. Brown rice syrup	1 tbsp (20g)	98
4. Cane sugar	1 tsp (4g)	65
5. Coconut sugar	1 tsp (4g)	35
6. Corn syrup	1 tbsp (20g)	75
7. Dextrose	1 tbsp (15g)	100

8.	Erythritol	1 tbsp (12g)	0
9.	Fructose	1 tsp (4g)	20-25
10.	Glucose	1 tsp (4g)	100
11.	High fructose corn syrup	1 tbsp (20g)	87
12.	Honey	1 tsp (7g)	55
13.	Inulin	1 tsp (3g)	0
14.	Isomalt	1 tsp (5g)	2
	Sweeteners	Weight	GI Value
15.	Lactitol	1 tsp (4g)	6
16.	Maltitol	1 tsp (4g)	35
17.	Maple syrup	1 tbsp (20g)	54
18.	Monk fruit extract	1 tsp (0.5g)	0
19.	Neotame	1 packet (0.3g)	0
20.	Palm sugar	1 tsp (4g)	35
21.	Raw sugar	1 tsp (4g)	65
22.	Saccharin	1 packet (0.1g)	0
23.	Sorbitol	1 tsp (4g)	9
24.	Splenda	1 packet (1g)	0
25.	Stevia	1 tsp (0.5g)	0
26.	Sucralose	1 packet (1g)	0
27.	Tagatose	1 tsp (4g)	3
28.	Treacle	1 tbsp (20g)	65
29.	Xylitol	1 tsp (4g)	13
30.	Allulose	1 tsp (4g)	0
31.	Yacon syrup	1 tsp (5g)	1
32.	Glycerol	1 tsp (5g)	5
33.	Fruit juice concentrates	1 tsp (10g)	varies
34.	Barley malt syrup	1 tbsp (20g)	42

35. Blackstrap molasses	1 tsp (7g)	55
36. Brown sugar	1 tsp (4g)	65
37. Date sugar	1 tsp (4g)	55
38. Grape sugar	1 tsp (4g)	100
39. Lactose	1 tsp (4g)	46
40. Maltodextrin	1 tsp (4g)	85
41. Molasses	1 tsp (7g)	55
Sweeteners	Weight	GI Value
42. Muscovado sugar	1 tsp (4g)	65
43. Raw honey	1 tsp (7g)	30
44. Rice malt syrup	1 tbsp (20g)	98
45. Sorghum syrup	1 tbsp (20g)	50
46. Syrup	1 tbsp (20g)	varies
47. Tapioca syrup	1 tbsp (20g)	85
48. White sugar	1 tsp (4g)	65
49. Yuzu sugar	1 tsp (4g)	65
50. Dried cane syrup	1 tsp (4g)	65
51. Galactose	1 tsp (4g)	100
52. Glucitol	1 tsp (4g)	2
53. Mannitol	1 tsp (4g)	0
54. Maple sugar	1 tsp (4g)	54
55. Raw agave nectar	1 tsp (5g)	10-19
56. Raw coconut nectar	1 tsp (4g)	35
57. Sucanat	1 tsp (4g)	65
58. Turbinado sugar	1 tsp (4g)	65
59. Black honey	1 tsp (7g)	30-50
60. Coconut nectar	1 tsp (4g)	35
61. Date syrup	1 tsp (7g)	42

62.	Evaporated cane juice	1 tsp (4g)	65
63.	Liquid cane sugar	1 tsp (4g)	65
64.	Lucuma powder	1 tsp (5g)	25
65.	Organic raw honey	1 tsp (7g)	30
66.	Organic sugar	1 tsp (4g)	65
67.	Panela	1 tsp (4g)	65
68.	Powdered sugar	1 tsp (4g)	65
	Sweeteners	Weight	GI Value
69.	Raw cane sugar	1 tsp (4g)	65
70.	Raw organic agave nectar	1 tsp (5g)	10-19
71.	Raw organic coconut nectar	1 tsp (4g)	35
72.	Stevia extracts	1 tsp (0.5g)	0
73.	Sweet sorghum syrup	1 tsp (7g)	50
74.	White grape sugar	1 tsp (4g)	100
75.	Birch sugar	1 tsp (4g)	0
76.	Caramel	1 tbsp (20g)	varies
77.	Crystalized honey	1 tsp (7g)	55
78.	Date molasses	1 tbsp (20g)	42
79.	Granulated sugar	1 tsp (4g)	65
80.	Invert sugar	1 tsp (4g)	100
81.	Liquid honey	1 tsp (7g)	55
82.	Lactitol	1 tsp (4g)	6
83.	Monin sugar-free sweetener	1 tsp (4g)	0
84.	Neotame	1 tsp (4g)	0
85.	Organic coconut sugar	1 tsp (4g)	35
86.	Organic date sugar	1 tsp (4g)	50
87.	Organic maple syrup	1 tbsp (20g)	54
88.	Organic palm sugar	1 tsp (4g)	35

89. Raw blue agave syrup	1 tsp (5g)	15
90. Raw cane syrup	1 tsp (4g)	65
91. Raw coconut sugar	1 tsp (4g)	35
92. Raw yacon syrup	1 tsp (4g)	1
93. Simple syrup	1 tbsp (20g)	varies
94. Sugar cane syrup	1 tbsp (20g)	65
95. Sugar in the raw	1 tsp (4g)	65
Sweeteners	Weight	GI Value
96. Xylitol	1 tsp (4g)	13
97. Zylitol	1 tsp (4g)	12
98. Tagatose	1 tsp (4g)	3
99. Allulose	1 tsp (4g)	0

Processed Foods And Their GI Values

Please note that the GI values and weights may vary depending on the specific brand and preparation method used.

Processed Foods	Weight	GI Value
1) White bread	30g	70
2) Bagel	105g	72
3) Croissant	57g	67
4) Muffin	60g	60
5) Pancake	75g	67
6) Waffles	75g	76
7) Cornflakes	30g	81
8) Rice Krispies	30g	82
9) Cheerios	30g	74

10)	Special K	30g	69
11)	Oatmeal	250g	58
12)	Granola	60g	55
13)	Fruit yogurt	100g	41
14)	Vanilla yogurt	100g	30
15)	Chocolate milk	250g	34
16)	Low-fat milk	250g	37
17)	Whole milk	250g	41
	Processed Foods	Weight	GI Value
18)	Soy milk	250g	34
19)	Almond milk	250g	25
20)	Apple juice	250g	40
21)	Orange juice	250g	50
22)	Cranberry juice	250g	68
23)	Grapefruit juice	250g	48
24)	Tomato juice	250g	38
25)	Ginger ale	250g	67
26)	Lemonade	250g	50
27)	Iced tea	250g	47
28)	Gatorade	250g	78
29)	Powerade	250g	70
30)	Coke	250g	63
31)	Sprite	250g	76
32)	Pepsi	250g	59
33)	Mountain Dew	250g	72
34)	Root beer	250g	52
35)	Red Bull	250g	63
36)	Monster	250g	65

	Weight	GI Value
37) 5-Hour Energy	60g	70
38) Pop-Tarts	50g	70
39) Ritz crackers	30g	85
40) Saltine crackers	30g	74
41) Wheat Thins	30g	67
42) Triscuits	30g	76
43) Cheese crackers	30g	85
44) Doritos	30g	72
Processed Foods	Weight	GI Value
45) Cheetos	30g	64
46) Fritos	30g	56
47) Lay's potato chips	30g	54
48) Pringles	30g	56
49) Cheese puffs	30g	67
50) Popcorn	30g	65
51) Beef jerky	30g	0
52) Pepperoni	30g	0
53) Hot dogs	60g	0
54) Ham	60g	0
55) Turkey	60g	0
56) Salami	30g	0
57) Bologna	30g	0
58) Chicken nuggets	100g	46
59) Chicken tenders	100g	46
60) Fish sticks	100g	59
61) Fish fillet	100g	46
62) Crab cakes	100g	47
63) Shrimp	100g	0

	Weight	GI Value
64) Lobster	100g	0
65) Clams	100g	0
66) Oysters	100g	0
67) Tuna salad	100g	0
68) Chicken salad	100g	0
69) Egg salad	100g	0
70) Macaroni and cheese	200g	64
71) Spaghetti	200g	42
Processed Foods	Weight	GI Value
72) Lasagna	200g	47
73) Pizza	100g	80
74) Cheeseburger	100g	61
75) Hamburger	100g	55
76) French fries	100g	75
77) Onion rings	100g	75
78) Chicken wings	100g	0
79) Chicken fingers	100g	0
80) Nachos	100g	72
81) Quesadilla	100g	50
82) Burrito	200g	44
83) Taco	100g	50
84) Enchilada	200g	49
85) Beef chili	200g	0
86) Chicken noodle soup	200g	48
87) Tomato soup	200g	38
88) Clam chowder	200g	0
89) Cream of mushroom soup	200g	0

		Weight	GI Value
90)	Beef stew	200g	0
91)	Shepherd's pie	200g	49
92)	Beef pot pie	200g	59
93)	Chicken pot pie	200g	53
94)	Veggie burger	100g	51
95)	Tofu	100g	0
96)	Seitan	100g	0
97)	Veggie hot dog	60g	69
98)	Veggie nuggets	100g	52
	Processed Foods	Weight	GI Value
99)	Falafel	100g	32
100)	Tempura	100g	71

Nuts And Their GI Values

	Nuts	Weight	GI Value
1.	Almonds	1 ounce (28g), +/- 5g	23
2.	Brazil nuts	1 ounce (28g), +/- 3g	15
3.	Cashews	1 ounce (28g), +/- 4g	22
4.	Chestnuts	1 ounce (28g), +/- 2g	54
5.	Hazelnuts	1 ounce (28g), +/- 3g	15
6.	Macadamia nuts	1 ounce (28g), +/- 4g	0
7.	Peanuts	1 ounce (28g), +/- 2g	14
8.	Pecans	1 ounce (28g), +/- 3g	0
9.	Pine nuts	1 ounce (28g), +/- 2g	15
10.	Pistachios	1 ounce (28g), +/- 3g	34
11.	Walnuts	1 ounce (28g), +/- 4g	15

	Nuts	Weight	GI Value
12.	Almonds	1/4 cup (30g), +/- 5g	23
13.	Brazil nuts	1/4 cup (30g), +/- 3g	15
14.	Cashews	1/4 cup (30g), +/- 4g	22
15.	Chestnuts	1/4 cup (30g), +/- 2g	54
16.	Hazelnuts	1/4 cup (30g), +/- 3g	15
17.	Macadamia nuts	1/4 cup (30g), +/- 4g	0
18.	Peanuts	1/4 cup (30g), +/- 2g	14
19.	Pecans	1/4 cup (30g), +/- 3g	0
20.	Pine nuts	1/4 cup (30g), +/- 2g	15
21.	Pistachios	1/4 cup (30g), +/- 3g	34
22.	Walnuts	1/4 cup (30g), +/- 4g	15
	Nuts	Weight	GI Value
23.	Almonds	1/2 cup (60g), +/- 5g	23
24.	Brazil nuts	1/2 cup (60g), +/- 3g	15
25.	Cashews	1/2 cup (60g), +/- 4g	22
26.	Chestnuts	1/2 cup (60g), +/- 2g	54
27.	Hazelnuts	1/2 cup (60g), +/- 3g	15
28.	Macadamia nuts	1/2 cup (60g), +/- 4g	0
29.	Peanuts	1/2 cup (60g), +/- 2g	14
30.	Pecans	1/2 cup (60g), +/- 3g	0
31.	Pine nuts	1/2 cup (60g), +/- 2g	15
32.	Pistachios	1/2 cup (60g), +/- 3g	34
33.	Walnuts	1/2 cup (60g), +/- 4g	15
34.	Almonds	1 cup (120g), +/- 5g	23
35.	Brazil nuts	1 cup (120g), +/- 3g	15
36.	Cashews	1 cup (120g), +/- 4g	22
37.	Chestnuts	1 cup (120g), +/- 2g	54
38.	Hazelnuts	1 cup (120g), +/- 3g	15

	Nuts	Weight	GI Value
39.	Macadamia nuts	1 cup (120g), +/- 4g	0
40.	Peanuts	1 cup (120g), +/- 2g	14
41.	Pecans	1 cup (120g), +/- 3g	0
42.	Pine nuts	1 cup (120g), +/- 2g	15
43.	Pistachios	1 cup (120g), +/- 3g	34
44.	Walnuts	1 cup (120g), +/- 4g	15
45.	Almond butter	2 tablespoons (32g), +/- 2g	0
46.	Brazil nut butter	2 tablespoons (32g), +/- 2g	0
47.	Cashew butter	2 tablespoons (32g), +/- 2g	27
48.	Hazelnut butter	2 tablespoons (32g), +/- 2g	17
49.	Macadamia nut butter	2 tablespoons (32g) +/- 2g	0
	Nuts	Weight	GI Value
50.	Peanut butter	2 tablespoons (32g), +/- 2g	14
51.	Pecan butter	2 tablespoons (32g), +/- 2g	0
52.	Pistachio butter	2 tablespoons (32g), +/- 2g	23
53.	Walnut butter	2 tablespoons (32g), +/- 2g	15
54.	Almond milk	1 cup (240ml), +/- 10ml	0
55.	Brazil nut milk	1 cup (240ml), +/- 10ml	0
56.	Cashew milk	1 cup (240ml), +/- 10ml	22
57.	Hazelnut milk	1 cup (240ml), +/- 10ml	15
58.	Macadamia nut milk	1 cup (240ml), +/- 10ml	0
59.	Peanut milk	1 cup (240ml), +/- 10ml	14
60.	Pecan milk	1 cup (240ml), +/- 10ml	0
61.	Pistachio milk	1 cup (240ml), +/- 10ml	34
62.	Walnut milk	1 cup (240ml), +/- 10ml	15
63.	Almond flour	1/4 cup (28g), +/- 2g	0
64.	Brazil nut flour	1/4 cup (28g), +/- 2g	0
65.	Cashew flour	1/4 cup (28g), +/- 2g	0

	Nuts	Weight	GI Value
66.	Chestnut flour	1/4 cup (28g), +/- 2g	65
67.	Hazelnut flour	1/4 cup (28g), +/- 2g	0
68.	Macadamia nut flour	1/4 cup (28g), +/- 2g	0
69.	Peanut flour	1/4 cup (28g), +/- 2g	30
70.	Pecan flour	1/4 cup (28g), +/- 2g	0
71.	Pistachio flour	1/4 cup (28g), +/- 2g	20
72.	Walnut flour	1/4 cup (28g), +/- 2g	0
73.	Almond meal	1/4 cup (28g), +/- 2g	0
74.	Brazil nut meal	1/4 cup (28g), +/- 2g	0
75.	Cashew meal	1/4 cup (28g), +/- 2g	0
76.	Hazelnut meal	1/4 cup (28g), +/- 2g	0
	Nuts	Weight	GI Value
77.	Macadamia nut meal	1/4 cup (28g), +/- 2g	0
78.	Peanut meal	1/4 cup (28g), +/- 2g	15
79.	Pecan meal	1/4 cup (28g), +/- 2g	0
80.	Pistachio meal	1/4 cup (28g), +/- 2g	20
81.	Walnut meal	1/4 cup (28g), +/- 2g	0
82.	Almond oil	1 tablespoon (15ml), +/- 1ml	0
83.	Brazil nut oil	1 tablespoon (15ml), +/- 1ml	0
84.	Cashew oil	1 tablespoon (15ml), +/- 1ml	0
85.	Hazelnut oil	1 tablespoon (15ml), +/- 1ml	0
86.	Macadamia nut oil	1 tablespoon (15ml), +/- 1ml	0
87.	Peanut oil	1 tablespoon (15ml), +/- 1ml	0
88.	Pecan oil	1 tablespoon (15ml), +/- 1ml	0
89.	Pistachio oil	1 tablespoon (15ml), +/- 1ml	0
90.	Walnut oil	1 tablespoon (15ml), +/- 1ml	0
91.	Mixed nuts	1 cup (120g), +/- 5g	0-30
92.	Nut trail mix	1 cup (120g), +/- 5g	0-30

93. Nut butter cookies 1 cookie (15g), +/- 1g   55-65
94. Nut granola   1/4 cup (30g), +/- 2g   55-70
95. Nut milk chocolate 1 bar (40g), +/- 2g   55-70
96. Nut protein bars   1 bar (40g), +/- 2g   50-65
97. Nut bread   1 slice (30g), +/- 1g   50-70
98. Nut butter fudge 1 piece (20g), +/- 1g   60-70
99. Nut butter energy bites 1 bite (10g), +/- 1g   55-65
100.Nut and fruit trail mix bars 1 bar (40g), +/- 2g 40-60

Beverages And Their GI Values

Beverages	Volume	GI Value
1) Water	500ml	0
2) Black coffee	250ml	0
3) Green tea	250ml	0
4) Herbal tea	250ml	0
5) Decaffeinated coffee	250ml	0
6) Decaffeinated black tea	250ml	0
7) Decaffeinated green tea	250ml	0
8) Coconut water	250ml	3
9) Tomato juice	250ml	38
10) Pineapple juice	250ml	46
11) Orange juice	250ml	50
12) Apple juice	250ml	40
13) Grape juice	250ml	59
14) Cranberry juice	250ml	68
15) Lemonade	250ml	74

16) Soda water	500ml	0
17) Mineral water	500ml	0
18) Almond milk	250ml	30
19) Soy milk	250ml	31
20) Skim milk	250ml	32
21) Whole milk	250ml	27
22) Chocolate milk	250ml	45
23) Orangeade	250ml	76
24) Lemon-lime soda	250ml	77
25) Ginger ale	250ml	80
26) Tonic water	250ml	89
Beverages	Volume	GI Value
27) Grapefruit juice	250ml	48
28) Carrot juice	250ml	43
29) Beetroot juice	250ml	64
30) Pomegranate juice	250ml	53
31) Mango juice	250ml	51
32) Guava juice	250ml	55
33) Kiwi juice	250ml	58
34) Grapefruit soda	250ml	76
35) Cream soda	250ml	80
36) Lemon-lime sports drink	250ml	65
37) Citrus sports drink	250ml	77
38) Energy drink	250ml	85
39) Malted milkshake	250ml	50
40) Vanilla milkshake	250ml	65
41) Strawberry milkshake	250ml	60
42) Chocolate milkshake	250ml	55

	Volume	GI Value
43) Vanilla soy milk	250ml	31
44) Chocolate soy milk	250ml	43
45) Vanilla almond milk	250ml	30
46) Chocolate almond milk	250ml	45
47) Rice milk	250ml	79
48) Oat milk	250ml	70
49) Caramel latte	250ml	47
50) Vanilla latte	250ml	40
51) Cappuccino	250ml	30
52) Americano	250ml	0
53) Espresso	50ml	0
Beverages	Volume	GI Value
54) Turkish coffee	50ml	0
55) Iced coffee	250ml	45
56) Iced tea	250ml	0
57) Hot chocolate	250ml	60
58) Chocolate milkshake	250ml	55
59) Orange smoothie	250ml	48
60) Blueberry smoothie	250ml	53
61) Mango smoothie	250ml	51
62) Strawberry smoothie	250ml	45
63) Grape smoothie	250ml	59
64) Banana smoothie	250ml	60
65) Vanilla protein shake	250ml	20
66) Chocolate protein shake	250ml	25
67) Strawberry protein shake	250ml	22
68) Green juice	250ml	29
69) Wheatgrass juice	30ml	0

	Volume	GI Value
70) Lemon water	250ml	0
71) Honey lemon water	250ml	55
72) Ginger water	250ml	0
73) Cranberry smoothie	250ml	68
74) Chocolate milk	250ml	45
75) Raspberry smoothie	250ml	40
76) Peach smoothie	250ml	56
77) Watermelon juice	250ml	72
78) Cantaloupe juice	250ml	65
79) Papaya juice	250ml	60
80) Carrot smoothie	250ml	43
Beverages	Volume	GI Value
81) Apple cider	250ml	36
82) Pineapple smoothie	250ml	46
83) Lemon-lime sparkling water	500ml	0
84) Coconut milk	250ml	50
85) Blackberry smoothie	250ml	39
86) Apricot juice	250ml	44
87) Kiwi smoothie	250ml	58
88) Mango lassi	250ml	33
89) Chocolate almond milkshake	250ml	50
90) Cucumber juice	250ml	15
91) Apple smoothie	250ml	40
92) Pear juice	250ml	38
93) Strawberry lemonade	250ml	74
94) Grapefruit sparkling water	500ml	0
95) Watermelon smoothie	250ml	72
96) Lemon ginger tea	250ml	0

97) Strawberry lemon smoothie 250ml		45
98) Pina colada smoothie 250ml		54
99) Mixed berry smoothie 250ml		50
100) Matcha latte 250ml		0

Herbs And Spices And Their GI Values

Herbs & Spices	Weight	GI Value
1. Allspice	1 tsp (2g)	0
2. Anise	1 tsp (2g)	0
3. Basil	1 tbsp (2g)	0

Herbs & Spices	Weight	GI Value
4. Bay leaves	1 tsp (1g)	0
5. Black pepper	1 tsp (2g)	0
6. Caraway	1 tsp (2g)	0
7. Cardamom	1 tsp (2g)	0
8. Cayenne pepper	1 tsp (2g)	0
9. Celery seeds	1 tsp (3g)	0
10. Chervil	1 tbsp (2g)	0
11. Chives	1 tbsp (3g)	0
12. Cilantro	1 tbsp (4g)	0
13. Cinnamon	1 tsp (2g)	0
14. Cloves	1 tsp (2g)	0
15. Coriander	1 tsp (2g)	0
16. Cumin	1 tsp (2g)	0
17. Curry powder	1 tsp (2g)	0

18. Dill	1 tsp (1g)	0
19. Fennel	1 tsp (2g)	0
20. Fenugreek	1 tsp (3g)	0
21. Garlic	1 clove (3g)	0
22. Ginger	1 tsp (2g)	0
23. Horseradish	1 tsp (5g)	0
24. Juniper berries	(1g)	0
25. Lavender	(1g)	0
26. Lemon balm	(1g)	0
27. Lemon grass	(1g)	0
28. Lemon peel	(1g)	0
29. Marjoram	(1g)	0
30. Mustard seeds	1 tsp (2g)	0
Herbs & Spices	Weight	GI Value
31. Nutmeg	1 tsp (2g)	0
32. Onion powder	1 tsp (2g)	0
33. Oregano	1 tsp (1g)	0
34. Paprika	1 tsp (2g)	0
35. Parsley	1 tbsp (4g)	0
36. Peppermint	1 tsp (1g)	0
37. Poppy seeds	1 tbsp (9g)	1
38. Rosemary	1 tsp (1g)	0
39. Saffron	1 tsp (0.5g)	0
40. Sage	1 tsp (1g)	0
41. Savory	1 tsp (1g)	0
42. Spearmint	1 tsp (1g)	0
43. Star anise	1 tsp (2g)	0
44. Tarragon	1 tsp (1g)	0

		Weight	GI Value
45.	Thyme	1 tsp (1g)	0
46.	Turmeric	1 tsp (2g)	0
47.	Vanilla bean	1 tsp (2g)	0
48.	White pepper	1 tsp (2g)	0
49.	Ajwain	1 tsp (2g)	0
50.	Asafoetida	1 tsp (3g)	0
51.	Black mustard seeds	1 tsp (2g)	0
52.	Cassia	1 tsp (2g)	0
53.	Chilli powder	1 tsp (2g)	0
54.	Cinnamon sticks	1 stick (2g)	0
55.	Clove powder	1 tsp (2g)	0
56.	Cumin seeds	1 tsp (2g)	0
57.	Dried ginger	1 tsp (2g)	0
	Herbs & Spices	Weight	GI Value
58.	Garlic powder	1 tsp (3g)	0
59.	Mace	1 tsp (2g)	0
60.	Mustard oil	1 tsp (4g)	0
61.	Onion flakes	1 tsp (2g)	0
62.	Paprika powder	1 tsp (2g)	0
63.	Red pepper flakes	1 tsp (2g)	0
64.	Sichuan pepper	1 tsp (2g)	0
65.	Sweet paprika	1 tsp (2g)	0
66.	White mustard seeds	1 tsp (2g)	0
67.	Adobo seasoning	1 tsp (2g)	0
68.	Annatto seeds	1 tsp (2g)	0
69.	Black cumin seeds	1 tsp (2g)	0
70.	Carom seeds	1 tsp (2g)	0
71.	Celery salt	1 tsp (3g)	0

72. Chaat masala	1 tsp (2g)	0
73. Chinese five spice	1tsp (2g)	0
74. Curry leaves	1 tbsp (2g)	0
75. Dill weed	1 tsp (1g)	0
76. Fennel seeds	1 tsp (2g)	0
77. Fenugreek seeds	1 tsp (2g)	0
78. Garam masala	1 tsp (2g)	0
79. Garlic flakes	1 tsp (3g)	0
80. Green cardamom pods	1 tsp (2g)	0
81. Ground coriander	1 tsp (2g)	0
82. Juniper berries	1 tsp (2g)	0
83. Kaffir lime leaves	1 tsp (1g)	0
84. Lemon balm	1 tsp (1g)	0
Herbs & Spices	Weight	GI Value
85. Lemon peel	1 tsp (1g)	0
86. Lime peel	1 tsp (1g)	0
87. Mustard powder	1 tsp (2g)	0
88. Nutmeg	1 tsp (2g)	0
89. Paprika	1 tsp (2g)	0
90. Peppermint	1 tsp (1g)	0
91. Pink peppercorns	1 tsp (2g)	0
92. Roasted cumin powder	1 tsp (2g)	0
93. Rose petals	1 tsp (1g)	0
94. Sichuan peppercorns	1 tsp (2g)	0
95. Smoked paprika	1 tsp (2g)	0
96. Sumac	1 tsp (2g)	0
97. Tandoori masala	1 tsp (2g)	0
98. Tellicherry peppercorns	1 tsp (2g)	0

| 99. | Vanilla extract | 1 tsp (5g) | 0 |
| 100. | Za'atar | 1 tsp (2g) | 0 |

How To Track Your Glycemic Load Using The Chart And How To Make Meal Plans

To measure your glycemic load and create a meal plan using the glycemic index food guide chart, take the following actions:

1. The meals you want to eat should be identified: Check the Glycemic Index of each food shown on the chart. Foods with a value of 70 or more are rated as high on the Glycemic Index and should be consumed in moderation, while those with a value of 55 or less are rated as low on the index and may be consumed more freely.

2. Multiply the Glycemic Index value by the number of grams of carbohydrates in the serving size of the meal you want to consume to determine the glycemic load. Then, multiply by 100 to obtain the glycemic load. The Glycemic Load, for instance, would be 15 if a product had a Glycemic Index of 50 and a serving size of 30 grams of carbohydrates. 4 decimal places

3. Make a menu plan: Choose foods low on the Glycemic Index to reduce your total Glycemic Load.

To make well-balanced and fulfilling meals, combine foods from many categories, such as grains, proteins, veggies, fruits, and vegetables.

4. Check your blood sugar levels: If you need to check your blood sugar levels due to diabetes or another medical condition, use the Glycemic Index Food Guide Chart to help you decide what to eat.

5. Change your diet gradually: If you're new to utilizing the Glycemic Index Food Guide Chart, make tiny dietary adjustments and add low-GI items over time. This can support the long-term development of wholesome behaviors that you can maintain.

6. Keep in mind that the Glycemic Index Food Guide Chart is only one tool you may use to assist you in choosing foods that are healthy for you to consume. While planning your meals, it's crucial to take other aspects into account as well, such as portion sizes, nutrient content, and general dietary patterns.

Chapter 5: Guidelines and Recipes for Healthy
Low-GI Diet

A Model Menu For Low GI

Using a range of low-GI foods in your meal plans will assist in maintaining steady blood sugar levels and give you long-lasting energy all day. As a starting point, consider the following sample low-GI food plan:

Breakfast:
- Oats with cinnamon and berries in 1/2 cup of cooked steel-cut oatmeal (GI value: 42, weight: 40g)
- a cooked egg (GI value: 0, weight: 50g)
- one little apple (GI value: 38, weight: 120g)

Breakfast treat:
- 1/4 cup of almonds (GI value: 0, weight: 28g)
- 1 little pear (GI value: 38, weight: 120g)

Lunch:
- Roasted veggies and grilled chicken breast with a mixed green salad (GI value: 15, weight: 100g)
- 0.5 cups of cooked quinoa (GI value: 53, weight: 80g)

Lunchtime nibbles:
- Half a cup of low-fat Greek yogurt with peach slices (GI value: 24, weight: 150g)

Dinner:
- Roasted sweet potato and salmon over grill with sautéed spinach (GI value: 17, weight: 150g)
- 1/4 cup cooked brown rice (GI value: 50, weight: 80g)

A late-night snack
- 1 cup of fresh berries (GI value: 40, weight: 70g)
- 1 little dark chocolate square (GI value: 23, weight: 10g)

Oats, quinoa, vegetables, fruits, and lean protein sources are just a few of the low-GI foods that are included in this example meal plan. These meals can help maintain stable blood sugar levels and offer continuous energy throughout the day.

It's crucial to keep in mind that every person's needs are different, and working with a registered dietitian or healthcare provider to develop a customized low-GI meal plan that suits your preferences and needs might be helpful.

100+ Low-GI Breakfast, Lunch, Dinner, And Snack Recipes

Finding meals and snacks that are enjoyable and tasty while yet adhering to the plan's rules is one of the problems of following a low-GI diet. Thankfully, there are many tasty, simple-to-make low-GI meals available. To assist you in making meal plans and achieving your low-GI eating objectives, we have selected 30 low-GI recipes, one for breakfast, lunch, supper, and snacks. These dishes show that consuming a low-GI diet doesn't require giving up flavor or enjoyment, from delicious omelets and robust soups to filling salads and delectable snacks.

30 Recipes For Breakfast

Sliced Almonds And Mixed Berries With Greek Yogurt

An appealing and nutrient-dense breakfast choice is Greek yogurt with a variety of berries and sliced almonds. This low-GI dish blends the creamy texture of Greek yogurt with the sweetness of mixed berries and the crunch of sliced almonds to provide a filling and wholesome breakfast.

Ingredients:

- one cup of unflavored Greek yogurt
- half a cup of mixed berries (strawberries, blueberries, raspberries, blackberries)
- One tablespoon of sliced almonds
- honey, 1 teaspoon (optional)

Instructions:

1. Add the Greek yogurt in its natural form to a small bowl.
2. Before adding them to the Greek yogurt dish, wash the mixed berries and chop them into bite-sized pieces.
3. The yogurt and berries should be covered with sliced almonds.
4. If you'd like, drizzle with honey.

An excellent approach to start your day on a healthy note is with this low-GI breakfast meal. Probiotics, which aid in better digestion and immune system support, are found in Greek yogurt and are good sources of protein, calcium, and other nutrients.

Berries are a great addition to any diet because of their low-calorie count and high levels of vitamins, antioxidants, and fiber. Sliced almonds give a gratifying crunch and good fats that can help you feel full and pleased all morning long.

Spinach, Tomato, And Feta Cheese Omelet With Vegetables

This is a tasty and healthy breakfast dish that is high in nutrients and low in GI is a veggie omelet with spinach, tomatoes, and feta cheese. Anybody looking to start the day with a nutritious and satisfying lunch should try this dish.

Ingredients:
- 3 eggs
- one-fourth cup of chopped spinach
- 25% of a cup of chopped tomatoes
- Feta cheese, chopped into 1/4 cup
- one tablespoon of olive oil
- salt and pepper

Instructions:

1. Sprinkled with salt and pepper, the eggs beaten in a basin.

2. A nonstick skillet with medium-high heat should be used to warm the olive oil.

3. For 1-2 minutes, add the spinach, stirring occasionally until wilted.

4. For a further 1-2 minutes, add the chopped tomatoes to the pan.

5. The veggies should simmer for 1-2 minutes after the beaten eggs are added.

6. Let the raw egg run below the omelet by gently lifting the edges with a spatula.

7. The feta cheese crumbles should be added to the omelet once the egg has cooked on one side.

8. In order to properly cook the eggs and melt the cheese, fold the omelet in half and cook it for an additional one to two minutes.

9. This tasty, nutritious veggie omelet is ready to be enjoyed when served hot!

Banana Slices And Unsweetened Coconut Flakes In a Chia Seed Pudding

Adding sliced banana and unsweetened coconut flakes to chia seed pudding makes for a tasty and healthy low-GI breakfast or snack. Chia seeds are a fantastic source of fiber, protein, and healthy fats. When paired with sliced banana and unsweetened coconut flakes, this dish makes a filling and delicious breakfast that will keep you feeling full and energized all morning. Making it is as follows:

Ingredients:
- Chia seeds, 1/4 cup
- a single cup of unsweetened almond milk
- 2 tablespoons of unsweetened coconut flakes
- 1 banana, cut into slices

Instructions:
1. Almond milk and chia seeds should be thoroughly mixed in a medium bowl.
2. After it thickens and the chia seeds have absorbed the liquid, let the mixture stand for at least 15 minutes, stirring every so often.
3. Spoon the thickened chia seed pudding into a dish or drink when it has thickened.
4. Sprinkle unsweetened coconut flakes and banana slices on top.

Feel free to add your preferred low-GI fruits, nuts, or seeds for more texture and taste to this recipe, which is highly adaptable.

Smoked Salmon, Arugula, And Avocado On Toast

An easy and tasty breakfast option is avocado toast, which can be tailored to your preferences and dietary requirements. To make a savory, satisfying lunch that is low on the glycemic index, this dish includes smoked salmon and arugula.

Ingredients:
- One piece of whole-grain bread
- Half an avocado
- 1/2 lemon
- 1 to 2 pieces of smoked salmon
- Arugula in small amounts
- Salt and pepper.

Instructions:
1. When desired, crisp up the bread piece in the toaster.
2. Avocado should be pitted and split in half while the bread is browning.
3. In a bowl, place the avocado's flesh that has been scooped out.
4. When the avocado has the consistency you like, squeeze half a lemon over it and mash it with a fork.
5. Add salt and pepper to taste before sprinkling the mashed avocado.
6. Spread the mashed avocado on top of the toast once it has cooled a bit.
7. Top the avocado with a few pieces of smoked salmon.
8. Arugula leaves should be added on top.

9. If you'd like more taste, add some unsweetened coconut flakes on top.

With healthy fats and protein to keep you satisfied and energized throughout the day, this low-GI breakfast is a fantastic way to start the day. Adding or changing ingredients to suit your preferences and tastes is another simple way to alter the recipe.

Sliced Apples, Cinnamon, And Walnuts Added To Steel-Cut Oats

It's simple to make a wonderful and nutritious breakfast choice with steel-cut oats, sliced apples, cinnamon, and chopped walnuts. Steel-cut oats are a fantastic low-GI alternative that provides you with long-lasting energy and supports your ability to feel full all morning long. Apples are a fruit with a low glycemic index (GI) and are a good source of fiber and antioxidants. Cinnamon helps control blood sugar. To this delectable breakfast meal, chopped walnuts bring wholesome fats and a delightful crunch.

Ingredients:
- Oats, steel sliced, in a cup
- two cups of water
- A single cup of unsweetened almond milk
- thinly cut apple, one

- 1 tsp. of cinnamon
- 1/fourth cup chopped walnuts

Instructions:

1. Almond milk and water should be heated over medium-high heat in a medium saucepan.
2. Heat should be turned down to low after adding the steel-chopped oats. The oats should be soft and most of the liquid should have been absorbed after 20 to 25 minutes of cooking, sometimes stirring.
3. Prepare the apple slices and walnuts for chopping while the oats are cooking.
4. Stir in the sliced apples and cinnamon when the oats have finished cooking. The apples should be warmed by cooking for a further 2 to 3 minutes.
5. Chop some walnuts, then divide the oats into dishes.

Almond Milk, Spinach, And Avocado In a Low-Carb Green Smoothie

Green smoothies with low carbohydrates are a fantastic way to start the day with a filling breakfast. In addition to having a low glycemic index, this dish is minimal in carbs. With spinach, avocado, and almond milk, prepare the following delectable green smoothie:

Ingredients:

- 1 cup of spinach
- half an avocado
- A single cup of unsweetened almond milk
- A serving of vanilla protein powder (optional)
- one-third cup of chia seeds (optional)
- As required, ice cubes

Instructions:
1. Blend the spinach, avocado, almond milk, chia seeds, and protein powder if using (if using).
2. Until creamy and smooth, blend at high speed.
3. Add additional ice cubes and blend again if the liquid is too thick.
4. Fill a glass with the smoothie, then sip it.

Fiber, protein, good fats, as well as a number of vitamins and minerals, are all abundant in this smoothie. You may eat it as a low-GI breakfast and it will keep you full and content until lunch. Adding other low-GI fruits or vegetables, such as berries or kale, to this dish will allow you to make it your own.

Whole Wheat Bread And Poached Eggs With Sautéed Mushrooms

Having a low-GI breakfast like poached eggs with sautéed mushrooms and whole wheat bread can help you stay full and content until lunch.

Ingredients:
- 2 eggs
- Slicing up a cup of mushrooms
- one tablespoon of olive oil
- 2 pieces of whole wheat bread.
- salt and pepper.

Instructions:

1. On medium heat, heat skillet up with olive oil. After the mushrooms are added, sauté them for 5 to 7 minutes, or until they are browned and soft.

2. Water should be poured into a medium saucepan and heated to a slow simmer.

3. One egg should be cracked into a cup or small bowl. Create a vortex in the saucepan's water by stirring it with a spoon. In the center of the vortex, carefully pour the egg. The egg white will more easily envelop the yolk with the aid of the moving water.

4. If the yolk is still runny but the white is set, continue cooking the egg for another 2 to 3 minutes. To extract the egg from the water and set it on a dish, use a slotted spoon.

5. The second egg should be treated similarly.

6. Bread pieces are toasted.

7. On top of the bread, arrange the sautéed mushrooms.

8. Every bread piece should have one poached egg on it.

9. According to taste, add salt and pepper.

Thanks to the eggs, whole wheat bread, and mushrooms in this low-GI breakfast meal, you're getting a decent dose of fiber and protein. Also, the heart-healthy omega-3 fatty acids from the poached eggs lend a nice touch.

Avocado, Black Beans, And Scrambled Eggs In a Quinoa Breakfast Bowl

A breakfast bowl made with quinoa is a healthy and satisfying way to begin the day. A grain abundant in fiber and other minerals, quinoa has a low GI and is high in protein. A wonderful and filling breakfast is created with this recipe's combination of quinoa, scrambled eggs, black beans, and avocado.

Ingredients:

- one cup of cooked quinoa
- 2 big eggs, scrambled
- 1/2 cup black beans, drained and rinsed,
- 1/2 avocado, sliced
- 1/4 red onion
- 1/4 cup fresh cilantro, minced,
- 1 lime juice
- salt and pepper.

Instructions:

1. As soon as the quinoa has finished cooking, set it aside.
2. Add a dash of salt and pepper to the eggs and whisk them in a small bowl.
3. The eggs are added to a nonstick pan that has been heated to medium-low. Scramble the eggs until they are set, stirring periodically. Dispose of.
4. Black beans and red onion should be cooked all the way through in a separate pan.
5. Divide the quinoa into two bowls before putting the bowl together. Black beans, diced avocado, cilantro, and scrambled eggs should be added as a garnish.
6. Salt and pepper to taste, then drizzle with lime juice.

Sliced Peaches And Honey-Drizzled Low-Fat Cottage Cheese

Simple and tasty low-GI breakfast options include low-fat cottage cheese topped with thinly sliced peaches and a sprinkle of honey. Peaches offer a naturally sweet flavor and a healthy serving of fiber, while cottage cheese is a great protein source. While the honey doesn't raise blood sugar levels, it offers a hint of sweetness. An instruction guide for making this delectable meal is provided below:

Ingredients:
- One-half cup of low-fat cottage cheese
- 1 medium peach, thinly sliced
- 1 teaspoon honey

Instructions:
1. A bowl should be filled with cottage cheese.
2. Top with the peaches, and cut into slices.
3. Add a honey drizzle.

In addition to having a low GI, this meal is also quick and simple to make, making it the ideal choice for mornings when you're pressed for time. You may use other low-GI fruits like berries or thinly sliced bananas for the peaches, making them very flexible.

With Fresh Fruit On The Side, Turkey Sausage, And Sweet Potato Hash

For breakfast, try this dish, which is both wholesome and tasty. The turkey sausage adds lean protein to keep you full and happy, while the sweet potato offers complex carbs with a low GI. A nice accompaniment to this savory dish is the fresh fruit on the side. To prepare sweet potato hash with turkey sausage and a serving of fresh fruit, follow these instructions:

Ingredients:
- 1 sweet potato, diced
- 2 sliced turkey sausages
- 1/2 chopped onion
- 1 diced red bell pepper
- 2 minced garlic cloves
- 1 tablespoon olive oil.
- salt and pepper
- fresh fruit

Instructions:

1. A big skillet with medium heat is used to warm the olive oil.
2. For 5-7 minutes, or until it begins to soften, add the cubed sweet potato.

3. The skillet should now include the turkey sausage, red bell pepper, onion, and garlic. The sausage should be browned and the veggies cooked through.
4. According to taste, add salt and pepper.
5. With a side of fresh fruit, serve the sweet potato hash.

Asparagus, Goat Cheese, And Roasted Red Peppers In a Veggie Frittata

An excellent and delectable low-GI food for lunch is a veggie frittata with roasted red peppers, asparagus, and goat cheese. Making a tasty and protein-rich supper out of frittatas is a terrific way to use up any leftover vegetables in your refrigerator. In addition to being dairy-free, this dish is also gluten-free and readily adaptable.

Ingredients:
- Roasted and chopped one red bell pepper
- 6 asparagus stalks, cut into pieces after trimming
- 8 big ovules
- 1/2 cup unsweetened almond milk or 1/4 cup milk
- goat cheese, shredded, 2 oz.
- 2 tablespoons of olive oil
- salt and pepper.

Instructions:
1. Your oven should be preheated at 375°F (190°C).

2. Combine the eggs, milk, salt, and pepper in a medium bowl by whisking everything together thoroughly.
3. A 10-inch nonstick oven-safe pan with medium-high heat is used to heat the olive oil in this recipe.
4. After adding it, sauté the asparagus for 3–4 minutes, or until it is tender.
5. For one more minute, add the roasted red peppers and continue to sauté.
6. As the edges begin to firm after 3–4 minutes of cooking, pour the egg mixture into the pan.
7. Place the pan in the preheated oven after sprinkling goat cheese on top of the eggs.
8. The frittata should be cooked through and the cheese should be melted and brown in color after baking for 12 to 15 minutes.
9. After taking it out of the oven, give it some time to cool.
10. Frittata should be served warm after being cut into wedges.

Fresh Blueberries, Greek Yogurt, And Pancakes Made With Almond Flour

A tasty and wholesome substitute for regular pancakes is those made with almond flour. These gluten-free, low-carb, protein- and healthy-fat-rich pancakes are made with almond flour. For a filling and low-GI breakfast, top them with blueberries that are in season and Greek yogurt.

Ingredients:
- 1 cup almond meal
- 1 teaspoon of baking soda
- 2 tablespoons honey
- 1/4 teaspoon salt
- 2 large eggs.
- Unsweetened almond milk in a quarter cup
- 1/3 cup vanilla extract
- 50% of a cup of fresh blueberries
- for serving, Greek yogurt

Instructions:

1. Almond flour, baking soda, and salt should be mixed together in a bowl. Blend thoroughly.
2. Almond milk, honey, eggs, and vanilla extract should all be thoroughly combined in a different bowl.
3. Stirring is required to fully incorporate the wet and dry mixtures.
4. Add the blueberries slowly and gently.
5. a nonstick griddle or skillet that has been preheated. The batter should be poured onto the skillet or griddle once it is hot using a 1/4 cup measuring cup.

6. Until the pancakes are golden brown and thoroughly cooked, cook for 2-3 minutes on each side.
7. Greek yogurt and extra blueberries should be added to the pancakes before serving.

Honey, Pistachios, And Grilled Grapefruit

This is a delicious and healthful breakfast option with a low GI is broiled grapefruit with honey and pistachios. It's a great option for hectic mornings because this recipe is quick and simple to make. Perfect flavor and texture harmony are produced by the tart grapefruit, sweet honey, and crunchy pistachios.

Ingredients:
- Halves of 1 grapefruit
- 10 grams of honey
- Chopped pistachios in two tablespoons

Instructions:
1. Set the broiler to its highest setting.
2. Place the cut-side-up grapefruit on a baking sheet after cutting it in half.
3. Each grapefruit half with honey.
4. On top of the honey, scatter chopped pistachios.
5. The pistachios and honey should bubble up on the grapefruit during the last three to five minutes it is under the broiler.

6. To serve right away, take the grapefruit out of the oven.
7. Reminder: You can microwave the honey-coated grapefruit for one to two minutes if you prefer it warm. This is an alternative to broiling.

Baked Egg Cups Topped With Cherry Tomatoes, Spinach, And Parmesan Cheese

Yummy and low-GI baked egg cups with spinach, cherry tomatoes, and Parmesan cheese are a great breakfast option for meal prepping. They can be made as follows:

Ingredients:
- 6 eggs
- 1/4 cup of milk
- A single cup of chopped baby spinach
- Halves half a cup of cherry tomatoes
- Parmesan cheese, grated, one-fourth cup
- Salt and pepper
- cooking sputter

Instructions:
1. 350°F (180°C) should be the oven's preheated temperature.
2. The eggs, milk, salt, and pepper should all be whipped together in a mixing bowl.
3. Use cooking spray to coat a muffin pan.

4. To evenly fill each muffin cup, distribute the chopped spinach and cherry tomatoes.
5. Around 3/4 of the way up each cup, pour the egg mixture over the vegetables.
6. Top off each egg cup with a little grated Parmesan cheese.
7. The egg cups should be baked for 20 to 25 minutes, or until set and lightly golden on top.
8. Before serving, give the egg cups a chance to cool.
9. For a quick meal option on busy mornings, try these baked egg cups. They can be kept in an airtight container in the fridge for up to 5 days.

Sliced Strawberries, Sugar-Free Whipped Cream, And Whole-Grain Waffles

Whole-grain waffles with sliced strawberries and sugar-free whipped cream are an excellent choice if you're looking for a low-GI breakfast option that still satisfies your sweet tooth. It's simple to prepare and contains ingredients that are rich in nutrients. Making it is as follows:

Ingredients:
- one cup of whole-wheat flour
- Baking powder, 1 tablespoon
- one tablespoon of sugar (or substitute)
- Almond milk, one cup

- 1/4 teaspoon of salt (or any other milk substitute)
- 1 egg
- 1 tbsp. of coconut oil
- strawberries, cut into 1 cup
- A half-cup of heavy cream
- 1 tsp. vanilla extract
- favorite sweetener (stevia, honey, or maple syrup)

Instructions:

1. Following the manufacturer's instructions, preheat your waffle maker.
2. Mix the salt, sugar, baking powder, and flour in a big bowl.
3. The coconut oil, almond milk, and egg should all be combined in different bowls.
4. The dry ingredients should be combined just by adding the wet ingredients and stirring.
5. Cook the waffles in accordance with the manufacturer's instructions after pouring the batter into the waffle maker.
6. Heavy cream, vanilla extract, and sweetener should be combined and whipped until soft peaks form in a medium bowl.
7. Strawberry slices and sugar-free whipped cream should be placed on top of the waffles before serving.

Because the waffles are made with whole grains and the whipped cream contains healthy fats, this low-GI breakfast is not only delicious but also filling and satisfying. Having a healthy, balanced breakfast is a great way to start the day.

A Side Of Mixed Greens And Scrambled Eggs With Smoked Salmon

A tasty and wholesome low-GI breakfast option is scrambled eggs with smoked salmon and a side of mixed greens. This breakfast will keep you satisfied and energized all morning long since it is high in protein and good fats.

Ingredients:
- 2 eggs
- sliced 2 oz. smoked salmon
- 100 ml of mixed greens
- Olive oil, 1 tbsp
- salt and pepper

Instructions:
1. The eggs should be combined with a little salt and pepper in a small bowl.
2. In a nonstick skillet, warm the olive oil over medium heat.
3. Add the eggs to the skillet and scramble them until they are fully cooked, stirring often.

4. Place the scrambled eggs on a platter after removing them from the pan.
5. Sliced smoked salmon is placed on top of the scrambled eggs.
6. Mix the greens in a different bowl with a drizzle of olive oil, some salt, and pepper.
7. Serve mixed greens on the side along with scrambled eggs and smoked salmon.

Scrambled Eggs, Black Beans, And Salsa In a Low-Carb Breakfast Tortilla

A quick and simple way to get your day started well is with low-carb breakfast burritos. Protein and fiber in this dish will help you feel satisfied and invigorated all morning long.

Ingredients:
- 2 big eggs
- Drained and rinsed 1/4 cup of black beans
- 1/4 cup of salsa
- Diced 1/4 of an avocado
- 2 tablespoons of grated cheddar cheese
- Two substantial collard green leaves stem
- Salt and pepper
- Spray for frying

Instructions:

1. The eggs, salt, and pepper should all be combined in a small bowl.
2. Cooking spray should be applied to a non-stick skillet before heating it up.
3. The eggs should be poured into the skillet and scrambled until fully cooked.
4. Stir in the black beans and salsa before adding the eggs to the pan.
5. Sliced cheddar cheese and chopped avocado are added after the heat has turned off.
6. Divide the egg mixture among the collard green leaves and arrange them flat.
7. Burritos should be securely rolled, with the sides tucked in as you proceed.

Almond Milk, Chia Seeds, And Peanut Butter In a Smoothie

A tasty and wholesome way to start the day is with this peanut butter and banana smoothie. It's loaded with protein, fiber, and healthy fats to keep you feeling full and satisfied, with the benefits of chia seeds and almond milk as additional bonuses.

Ingredients:
- 1 banana that is fully ripe.
- natural peanut butter, 1 tbsp

- A serving of chia seeds
- unsweetened almond milk, 1 cup
- 1 or 2 ice cubes (optional)

Instructions:
1. Banana chunks should be tiny after being peeled.
2. Blender ingredients: banana, peanut butter, chia seeds, almond milk, and ice cubes (if using).
3. Mix until well-combined and creamy.
4. Put the smoothie in a glass and sip on it.

Optional: You may either freeze the banana in advance or add extra ice cubes to make the smoothie thicker. A scoop of vanilla protein powder can also be added for an additional protein boost.

Oats In The Oven With Apples And Cinnamon

For people who enjoy warm, substantial, and satisfying meals, baked oatmeal with apples and cinnamon is the ideal breakfast. This dish is simple to make and may be made ahead of time and kept in the refrigerator for a few days. In addition to having a low glycemic index, this meal is also rich in fiber, protein, and good fats, which will keep you full and happy until lunch.

Ingredients:
- Rolling oats in two cups

- 1/2 cup of apple slices
- 1/4 cup finely chopped walnuts
- 1/fourth cup raisins
- cinnamon, one teaspoon
- 1/3 tsp. nutmeg
- Unsweetened almond milk in two cups
- 2 eggs
- Maple syrup, two tablespoons
- 1/4 teaspoon salt, 1 teaspoon vanilla essence

Instructions:
1. Achieve a 375°F (190°C) oven temperature.
2. The baking dish should be 8 inches square.
3. The rolled oats, diced apples, walnuts, raisins, cinnamon, and nutmeg should all be combined in a big bowl.
4. Almond milk, eggs, maple syrup, vanilla extract, and salt should all be combined in a different bowl.
5. Combine the dry ingredients with the liquid components after adding them.
6. Place the prepared baking dish with the mixture inside.
7. Oatmeal should be set and the top should be golden brown after 35 to 40 minutes of baking.
8. Prior to serving, let it cool for a while.
9. Warm baked oatmeal should be served with a dollop of maple syrup, some Greek yogurt, or sliced bananas on top. The leftovers can be placed in the

fridge for up to 4 days, then reheated in the microwave or oven before serving.

Breakfast Quesadilla With Low-Fat Cheese, Black Beans, And Scrambled Eggs

A perfect way to start your day with a low-GI meal is with this breakfast quesadilla. To keep you feeling full and energized throughout the morning, it is packed with protein, fiber, and healthy fats. A balance of nutrients is provided by the mix of scrambled eggs, black beans, and low-fat cheese, while the whole-grain tortilla maintains a low GI value. This dish is perfect for hectic mornings since it comes together quickly and simply. Let's start with the recipe.

Ingredients:
- 1 tortilla whole-grain
- Scrambled two eggs
- 1/4 cup washed and drained black beans from a can
- 1/4 cup low-fat cheese crumbles
- 1/4 cup of salsa
- One tablespoon of fresh cilantro, chopped (optional)

Instructions:
1. Over medium heat, preheat a large nonstick skillet. To gently brown the tortilla, place it in the skillet and cook for 1 to 2 minutes on each side.

2. Scramble the eggs in a separate pan over medium heat until fully done.
3. On one side of the tortilla, spread the scrambled eggs. Top with salsa, shredded cheese, and black beans.
4. To make a quesadilla, fold the tortilla in half. After the cheese is melted and the tortilla is crispy, cook for a further 1-2 minutes on each side.
5. If preferred, garnish the heated dish with fresh cilantro.
6. For a healthy and filling breakfast, enjoy your low-GI quesadilla with a side of fresh fruit.

Banana Slices And Almond Butter On a Whole Wheat English Muffin

When you're in a rush in the mornings and want something quick and filling, this straightforward and healthy meal is ideal. Toasted to perfection, a whole wheat English muffin is topped with sweet, thin slices of banana and creamy almond butter. This breakfast's blend of nutritious grains, lean protein, and good fats is not only tasty but also filling and energizing.

Ingredients:
• A single whole-wheat English muffin
• One spoonful of almond butter
• Banana, cut in half.

Instructions:

1. Depending on how crisp you like your toast, toast the whole wheat English muffin.
2. On the toasted English muffin, spread the almond butter equally across both /halves.
3. A sliced banana is placed on one side of the English muffin.
4. To make a sandwich, top it with the remaining English muffin half.

Granola And Mixed Berries On a Low-Fat Greek Yogurt Parfait

Greek yogurt is a filling, protein-rich food that may be a wonderful foundation for a balanced breakfast. It makes a delightful and filling parfait with nutty granola and luscious berries that will keep you energized all morning. A recipe for a granola-topped, low-fat Greek yogurt parfait with mixed berries is provided below:

Ingredients:
- Greek yogurt low in fat, 1 cup
- 1/3 cup of granola
- 1/2 cup of mixed berries (such as strawberries, blueberries, and raspberries)
- 1 teaspoon honey (optional)

Instructions:

1. Greek yogurt and honey (if used) should be well mixed in a bowl before serving.
2. Yogurt, granola, and mixed berries should be layered in a serving glass or container.
3. To finish, add a layer of mixed berries on top once you've used up all the ingredients.
4. You may either serve right away or cover and store for later.

Low-Fat Cheese, Spinach, And Mushrooms In An Egg White Omelet

A tasty and nutritious breakfast choice that is simple to make is an egg white omelet with mushrooms, spinach, and low-fat cheese. Spinach and mushrooms are rich in vitamins and minerals, while egg whites are a fantastic source of protein. Without adding too many calories or bad fats, low-fat cheese enhances the taste. A spinach, mushroom, and low-fat cheese egg white omelet can be made by following these steps:

Ingredients:
- Three egg whites
- 1/2 cup of spinach leaves
- 1 cup of sliced mushrooms
- A quarter cup of low-fat cheese, shredded
- Salt and pepper.

- Cooking sputter

Instructions:

1. In a nonstick skillet, heat the oil to medium-high.
2. Add frying spray to the skillet.
3. When the veggies are soft, add the spinach and mushrooms to the pan and cook for a further 1-2 minutes.
4. Add salt and pepper to taste, then beat the egg whites in a small bowl.
5. Vegetables in the skillet should be covered with egg whites.
6. Once the omelet's bottom is set, cook for 2 to 3 minutes.
7. On top of the omelet, sprinkle the low-fat cheese shreds.
8. Flip the omelet over using a spatula.
9. To melt the cheese and fully cook the egg whites, heat for an additional 1-2 minutes.

Avocado Slices And Scrambled Eggs On Top Of Cauliflower Fried Rice

Cauliflower fried rice with scrambled eggs, sliced avocado, and low-carb, low-GI foods are the perfect low-carb, high-protein breakfast. Because of its high protein content, beneficial fats, and nutrient-dense vegetables, this meal is ideal for individuals who follow a ketogenic or paleo diet. Also, it's a fantastic way to utilize any leftover cauliflower rice from the previous evening!

Ingredients:
- 1 serving of cauliflower rice
- Whisked 2 eggs
- 1 cup of sliced mushrooms
- Onion dice, half a cup
- Bell peppers, diced, in a cup
- 1 minced clove of garlic
- 1 tablespoon coconut oil
- Avocado, cut in half.
- Salt and pepper.

Instructions:

1. Over a medium-high flame, warm the coconut oil in a skillet.
2. When the onions are finished, remove them from the heat.
3. Cook for a further 3–4 minutes after adding the bell peppers, mushrooms, and garlic.
4. Cauliflower rice should be cooked thoroughly after being added and cooked for 3 to 4 minutes.

5. Whisked eggs are added to the opposite side of the pan after the cauliflower rice and vegetables are pushed to one side.
6. Mix the cauliflower rice, vegetables, and completely cooked eggs in a scrambled state.
7. According to taste, add salt and pepper.
8. Avocado slices are placed on top and served hot.

A Poached Egg And Sliced Avocado On Whole-Grain Bread

Start your day off right with a tasty and uncomplicated breakfast using this recipe. As a tasty and filling addition, properly poached eggs and a creamy avocado over whole grain bread serve as a nutritious basis. Making it a flexible and filling supper, the recipe can readily be modified with your own toppings or seasonings.

Ingredients:
- 2 pieces of whole-grain bread
- 1 ripe avocado
- 2 eggs
- Salt and pepper.
- White vinegar, 1 teaspoon
- Red pepper flakes, tomato slices, and chopped herbs are optional garnishes.

Instructions:

1. You can crisp up the toast whatever you like.
2. In a small dish, scoop the avocado flesh after cutting it in half and removing the pit. Use a fork to mash the avocado, then season with salt & pepper to taste.
3. Bring a pot to a low simmer by adding about 2 inches of water to it. Include the vinegar.
4. Into a little bowl, crack one egg. The egg should be carefully placed in the center of the whirlpool you just made in the boiling water using a spoon. The egg whites should be set and the yolk remains runny after 3 to 4 minutes of cooking. The egg should be taken out of the water using a slotted spoon and placed on a towel to drain. The second egg should then be used.
5. Each slice of bread should have an avocado spread on it. Add a poached egg on the top of every slice. Sliced tomatoes, red pepper flakes, or chopped fresh herbs are a few optional toppings you may use.

Almond Flour And Coconut Oil Low-Carb Blueberry Muffins

This is a great option for those watching their carb intake is low-carb blueberry muffins made with almond flour and coconut oil. For those searching for a low-carb, gluten-free, and paleo-friendly breakfast option, this recipe is ideal.

Almond flour, coconut oil, eggs, vanilla extract, baking powder, salt, and fresh blueberries are all ingredients needed to make these muffins. After combining the ingredients, a muffin tin is filled with the mixture, which is baked until golden brown. These moist, tender muffins are loaded with juicy blueberries. The following steps will show you how to make low-carb blueberry muffins using almond flour and coconut oil:

Ingredients:
- 2 cups almond meal
- 1/4 cup melted coconut oil
- 3 large eggs
- 1 tablespoon vanilla extract
- 1 teaspoon baking powder
- Fresh blueberries and 1/4 teaspoon of salt

Instructions:

1. Turn on the oven to 350°F (180°C). Put paper liners in a muffin tin.
2. Almond flour, baking soda, and salt should be mixed together in a bowl.
3. The eggs, melted coconut oil, and vanilla extract should all be combined in a different mixing bowl.
4. Stir until thoroughly combined after adding the dry ingredients to the wet ones.
5. Add the blueberries with a little fold.

6. Fill each cup in the muffin pan with about 3/4 of the batter.
7. Until golden brown and a toothpick inserted into the center of a muffin comes out clean, bake for 20 to 25 minutes.
8. Before removing the muffins from the muffin tin, give them some time to cool. Warm or room temperature serving is recommended.

Greek Yogurt And Mixed Berries With Homemade Granola

Making homemade granola ahead of time so you can enjoy it all week long is a healthy and delectable breakfast option. Granola is a fantastic low-GI breakfast option because you can control how much sugar and fat it contains by making your own. For a well-rounded breakfast that will keep you full until lunch, combine it with Greek yogurt and mixed berries, which add protein, fiber, and antioxidants.

Ingredients:
- 3 cups of rolled old-fashioned oats
- A cup of chopped raw almonds
- A cup of chopped raw cashews
- A cup of unsweetened shredded coconut.
- Melted 1/4 cup coconut oil
- 1/4 cup honey

- 1 tablespoon vanilla extract
- 1/8 teaspoon of ground cinnamon
- Sea salt, 1/4 teaspoon
- One cup of mixed berries
- Greek yogurt, plain, one cup

Instructions:

1. Achieve a 325°F (165°C) oven temperature.
2. Combine the rolled oats, chopped cashews, chopped almonds, and coconut shreds in a sizable mixing bowl.
3. Mix the honey, melted coconut oil, vanilla, cinnamon powder, and sea salt in a separate mixing bowl.
4. When you've evenly coated the dry ingredients, pour the honey mixture over them and stir.
5. On a parchment-lined baking sheet, distribute the mixture evenly.
6. When the granola is fragrant and golden brown, bake for 25 to 30 minutes, stirring the mixture every 10 minutes.
7. Remove the baking sheet from the oven and let the granola cool completely.
8. Once it has cooled, the granola should be kept in an airtight container until needed.
9. To assemble, divide the Greek yogurt among 4 bowls, add a 1/2 cup of mixed berries to each, and top with 1/4 cup of homemade granola.

Scrambled Eggs, Turkey Bacon, And Sweet Potatoes In a Breakfast Skillet

This is a tasty and satisfying option for breakfast that can be prepared with a variety of ingredients. This recipe's high-protein, the low-carb meal will keep you full and energized all morning long because it includes sweet potatoes, turkey bacon, and scrambled eggs.

Ingredients:
- 1 big sweet potato, diced and peeled
- 4 slices of turkey bacon
- 4 large eggs, whisked together with a half teaspoon of smoked paprika
- Salt and pepper
- 1 teaspoon of olive oil
- Garnishing with chopped parsley

Instructions:
1. Achieve a 375°F oven temperature.
2. Over medium heat, warm the olive oil in a sizable oven-safe skillet.
3. In a skillet, combine the sweet potato and turkey bacon. Cook for 5 to 7 minutes, or until the sweet potato is soft and the turkey bacon is crisp.
4. Salt, pepper, and smoked paprika are used for seasoning.

5. Over the sweet potato and turkey bacon mixture, pour the whisked eggs and cook for 1-2 minutes.
6. When the eggs are set, place the skillet in the oven and bake for 10 to 15 minutes.
7. Before serving, remove from the oven and let cool for a while.
8. Enjoy with a sprinkle of chopped parsley on top!

Tomato Sauce And Poached Eggs In a Shakshuka

Poached eggs in a hot tomato sauce are the main ingredient in the popular Middle Eastern and North African dish shakshuka. It takes just a few easy steps to prepare this flavorful and nutritious breakfast. For a Shakshuka recipe, see,

Ingredients:
• 1 teaspoon of olive oil
• 1 sliced onion
• Minced three garlic cloves
• 1 chopped red bell pepper
• 1 can (14 oz) chopped tomatoes
• Two teaspoons of paprika
• 1 tsp. of cumin
• Cayenne pepper, 1/4 teaspoon
• Salt and pepper
• 4-6 eggs
• Chopped fresh cilantro or parsley as a garnish

Instructions:

1. In a big pan over medium heat, warm the olive oil. For about 5 minutes, add the chopped onions and sauté until soft.

2. Sauté for an additional two to three minutes before adding the minced garlic and red bell pepper.

3. Add salt, pepper, cayenne pepper, paprika, cumin, and a can of diced tomatoes. When the sauce has thickened, stir everything together and simmer for about 5 minutes.

4. Make small wells in the sauce with a spoon, and break the eggs into the wells. Once the eggs are cooked to your preference, cover the skillet and let it cook for an additional 5-7 minutes.

5. When the eggs are done, turn off the heat and sprinkle some chopped fresh parsley or cilantro on top.

6. Serve hot with pita or crusty bread.

Berries In a Mason Jar With Low-Fat Cottage Cheese

The quick and simple breakfast or snack option of low-fat cottage cheese and mixed berries in a mason jar is filling and healthy. For an easy grab-and-go meal, this recipe only requires minimal preparation.

Ingredients:
- 1 cup of cottage cheese with less fat
- One cup of mixed berries (strawberries, blueberries, raspberries)
- Honey, one tablespoon (optional)

Instructions
1. Set aside the rinsed mixed berries.
2. Low-fat cottage cheese should be thoroughly combined with honey (if using) in a bowl.
3. Fill the mason jar's bottom with half of the cottage cheese mixture.
4. On top of the cottage cheese, spread a layer of mixed berries.
5. Top the mixed berries with the remaining cottage cheese mixture by spoonfuls.
6. On top of the cottage cheese, spread out another layer of mixed berries.
7. Refrigerate the contents of the mason jar until you are ready to eat it.

Note: You can alter this recipe by substituting different berries for the ones called for, or by including nuts or seeds for more texture and flavor.

30 Recipes For Lunch

Salad Made With Grilled Chicken, Vegetables, And a Drizzle Of Oil

Olive oil-dressed grilled chicken and vegetables make a delicious and nutritious lunch or supper dish. The chicken and veggies are made soft and juicy by grilling them, and the rich and tangy flavor of the olive oil dressing complements this. For those following a low-carb diet, this salad is a fantastic choice because it is also low in carbohydrates and high in protein. Making it is as follows:

Ingredients:
- 2 chicken breasts without the bones or the skin.
- 2 tablespoons of olive oil
- 1 red bell pepper
- 1 yellow bell pepper
- 1 zucchini
- 1 red onion sliced
- Salt and pepper
- Greens in various combinations
- Kalamata olives, cherry tomatoes, and cucumbers cut in half
- Fata cheese
- As for the dressing: 2 tablespoons red wine vinegar
- 1 teaspoon honey

- 1 chopped garlic clove
- Salt and pepper to taste
- 1/4 cup olive oil.

Instructions:

1. The heat should be set to medium-high on the grill or grill pan.
2. Olive oil and salt and pepper should be used to season the chicken breasts.
3. The chicken breasts should be cooked through after 6 to 8 minutes on each side of the grill.
4. Sprinkle the sliced veggies with salt, pepper, olive oil, and other seasonings as the chicken cooks.
5. The veggies should be cooked through and mildly browned after grilling for 5 to 7 minutes, occasionally tossing them.
6. Combine olive oil, red wine vinegar, honey, garlic, salt, and pepper in a small bowl to prepare the dressing.
7. Griddled chicken, grilled veggies, cherry tomatoes, cucumber, kalamata olives, and feta cheese should be added to a bed of mixed greens before the salad is finished. Serve immediately after drizzling with the olive oil dressing.

Bread Made With Nutritious Grains And Lentil Soup

Lunch or supper can be served with lentil soup, which is a nutritious and filling dish. An excellent supplement to any plant-based diet, lentils are a fantastic source of protein and fiber. On a chilly winter day, this dish for lentil soup is the ideal comfort food.

Ingredients:
- One cup of drained and washed lentils
- 4 cups of vegetable broth
- 1 onion
- 3 cloves of minced garlic
- 2 carrots
- 2 stalks of celery
- Diced tomatoes in one can
- 1/tsp dried thyme
- Salt and pepper
- whole-grain bread.

Instructions:

1. Over medium heat, warm up some oil in a big saucepan. For about 5 minutes after adding, sauté the onion and garlic until they are tender.
2. For an additional 5 minutes, simmer the carrots and celery in the saucepan.
3. Lentils, vegetable broth, diced tomatoes, thyme, salt, and pepper should all be added to the saucepan.

Bring to a boil, then lower the heat and simmer the lentils for 30 to 40 minutes, depending on how tender you want your lentils.
4. Warm whole-grain bread should be served alongside the lentil soup.

Steamed Lettuce With Tuna Salad

An energizing and low-carb lunch option that takes only a few minutes to make is tuna salad lettuce wraps. A crisp lettuce leaf is used to wrap around the meal, which also calls for canned tuna, crunchy vegetables, and a tangy vinaigrette. Making it is as follows:

Ingredients:
• Two drained cans of tuna
• Red onion, celery, and bell pepper, each in a quarter cup, each diced
• A quarter cup of plain Greek yogurt
• Dijon mustard, 1 tablespoon
• Juice of one tablespoon of lemon
• Salt and pepper.
• Green lettuce

Instructions:
1. The diced red onion, celery, bell pepper, and drained tuna should all be combined in a mixing dish.

2. Greek yogurt, Dijon mustard, lemon juice, salt, and pepper should all be mixed together in a separate bowl.
3. The tuna mixture will be well-coated when the dressing has been added, so whisk it in.
4. The tuna salad should be placed in the middle of a lettuce leaf.
5. As you proceed, tuck the edges of the lettuce into the tuna salad to form a burrito-like wrap.
6. Add the remaining lettuce leaves and tuna salad thereafter.
7. Save in the refrigerator for later use or serve right away.

Mixed Green Salad, Broccoli, And Cheddar Soup

A filling lunch or dinner can be served with broccoli and cheddar soup, a tasty and substantial soup. While the broccoli offers a lot of fiber and minerals, the addition of cheddar cheese gives it a rich and creamy texture. This dinner is filling and healthy when it is served with a straightforward mixed green salad.

Ingredients:
- one tablespoon of olive oil
- Diced 1 onion
- Garlic, minced from two cloves
- 4 cups minced broccoli

- 4 cups chicken or veggie broth 1 cup grated cheddar cheese
- Salt and pepper
- Four cups of mixed greens
- One tablespoon of olive oil
- Juice of one tablespoon of lemon

Instructions:

1. Olive oil is heated over medium-low heat in a big saucepan. It takes around 5 minutes for the onion to become translucent after you add the chopped onion and minced garlic.

2. Add the chopped broccoli to the saucepan along with the chicken or veggie stock. Bring to a boil, then turn down the heat and simmer the soup for 10 to 15 minutes, or until the broccoli is soft.

3. Blend the soup with an immersion blender or in a blender after transferring it. Stir the shredded cheddar cheese into the soup once it has been added back to the saucepan, melting it completely. According to taste, add salt and pepper.

4. In a big bowl, combine the mixed greens with olive oil, lemon juice, salt, and pepper to make the mixed green salad.

5. A dish of mixed green salad should be served alongside the hot broccoli and cheddar soup.

Roasted Veggies And Fish On The Grill

A tasty and wholesome dish that is bursting with flavor and nutrients is grilled salmon with roasted veggies. Salmon is an excellent amount of omega-3 fatty acids, which are vital for both heart and brain health. Roasted veggies are a fantastic combination of fiber, vitamins, and minerals. In just 30 minutes, you can have this dinner ready because of how simple it is to make. The preparation of grilled salmon with roasted veggies is described in this step-by-step tutorial.

Ingredients:
- Four salmon fillets
- 2 tablespoons of olive oil
- 1 tablespoon of lemon juice
- Garlic powder, 1 teaspoon
- Salt and pepper
- Sliced red onion
- 2 tablespoons balsamic vinegar
- 1 red bell pepper, 2 zucchini
- 1 red bell pepper
- Two tablespoons of honey

Instructions:

1. Set the oven's temperature to 400 °F (200 °C).

2. Lemon juice, garlic powder, salt, and pepper should all be combined with 1 tablespoon of olive oil in a small bowl. Onto the salmon fillets, rub the mixture.

3. Using a medium-high heat source, preheat a grill pan. When it's heated, add the salmon fillets and cook them for approximately 3–4 minutes on each side, or until the fish is well cooked.

4. Sliced zucchini, red bell pepper, and red onion are combined with one tablespoon of olive oil, balsamic vinegar, honey, salt, and pepper while the salmon cooks.

5. On a baking sheet, spread out the veggies in a single layer. Roast the vegetables for 20 to 25 minutes, or until they are soft and have a light browning.

6. Together with the roasted veggies, plate the grilled salmon fillets.

7. Chop some fresh herbs, such as parsley or basil, as a garnish if desired to add flavor.

Vegetable Salad With Chickpeas

A nutritious lunch full of protein, fiber, and minerals is a chickpea and roasted veggie salad. You may add your own vegetables and herbs to this simple vegetarian salad to make it your own.

Ingredients:
- One can of drained and rinsed chickpeas
- A cup of cherry tomatoes, halved
- One red onion, chopped
- A red bell pepper, chopped
- A zucchini, chopped
- A yellow squash, chopped.
- Olive oil, 2 tablespoons
- 1-tablespoon balsamic vinegar
- One teaspoon of dried oregano
- Black pepper and salt as desired.
- Two cups of mixed greens

Instructions:

1. Your oven should be preheated to 400°F (200°C).
2. Chickpeas, red onions, red bell peppers, zucchini, yellow squash, cherry tomatoes, garlic, olive oil, balsamic vinegar, dried oregano, salt, and black pepper should all be combined in a big bowl. Mix

everything until the seasonings are evenly distributed throughout the vegetables.

3. The vegetables should be tender and lightly browned after roasting for 25 to 30 minutes in a preheated oven after being spread out evenly on a baking sheet.

4. Put your mixed greens in a sizable salad bowl and get started on the roasting vegetables.

5. Take the vegetables out of the oven when they are finished cooking and set them aside to cool.

6. The mixed greens should now have the roasted vegetables added to them. Combine everything thoroughly.

7. A salad of roasted vegetables and chickpeas should be served right away.

Veggies And Avocado On a Whole-Wheat Turkey Wrap

A satisfying lunch option that is healthy and filling is a whole-grain turkey wrap with avocado and vegetables. It's ideal for people who want to eat well and maintain their fitness goals. The avocado, whole grains, and vegetables in this wrap are high in fiber and contain lean protein from the turkey as well as healthy fats.

You'll need the following supplies to make this wrap:

*   1 wrap with whole grain

- several slices of turkey breast
- 1/4 of sliced avocado
- 1/fourth cup of chopped lettuce
- 1/fourth cup of sliced tomatoes
- 1/4 cup of sliced cucumber
- 1 teaspoon hummus
- Salt and pepper.

Instructions:

1. To begin, reheat the tortilla wrap for a total of 10 seconds in the microwave or for up to two minutes on a pan.
2. The tortilla wrap should have hummus on it.
3. Spread the hummus on a plate and top it with slices of turkey, avocado, lettuce, tomatoes, and cucumber.
4. According to taste, add salt and pepper.
5. Fold the sides in as you roll up the wrap tightly.
6. When ready to serve, split the wrap in half.

Tomato Sauce, Grilled Chicken, And Zucchini Noodles

When compared to traditional pasta, zucchini noodles, or "zoodles," are a delicious and healthy substitute. They are low in calories, high in fiber, and nutrient-dense because they are made from spiralized zucchini. A tasty and filling meal, this dish is served with grilled chicken and a flavorful tomato sauce.

Ingredients:
- Two medium zucchini
- One tablespoon of olive oil
- Minced two garlic cloves
- 1 can (14.5 ounces) tomatoes in dice
- A tsp. of dried oregano
- Salt and pepper.
- Grated Parmesan cheese
- Grilled chicken breasts totaling two breasts (optional)

Instructions:
1. Make zucchini noodles by spiralizing or peeling vegetables, then reserving.
2. Over medium heat, a pan is heating up with olive oil. Sauté the minced garlic for a couple of minutes until fragrant.
3. Salt, pepper, and diced tomatoes are all optional additions. Heat should be increased until the mixture is at a boil, then lowered. 15–20 minutes of simmering.
4. Cook chicken breasts on the grill until done while the tomato sauce is simmering. Make strips by slicing.
5. A little olive oil should be heated on medium heat in a different pan. Zucchini noodles are added, and they are cooked for 2–3 minutes, until tender.

6. Put the zucchini noodles in a bowl or plate and put the dish together. Sprinkle grilled chicken with tomato sauce on top.
7. Serve immediately and top with freshly grated Parmesan cheese.

Avocado, Salsa, And Black Beans In a Quinoa Bowl.

A tasty, nutritious, and simple vegetarian meal is a quinoa and black bean bowl with avocado and salsa. Quinoa is a grain rich in nutrients and high in protein and fiber, and black beans add even more protein and fiber to the dish along with vital vitamins and minerals. The dish gets a boost of flavor from the salsa and a healthy dose of fats from the avocado.

Ingredients:
- One can of rinsed and drained black beans
- One ripe avocado, cut into slices
- Half a cup of salsa.
- One cup of rinsed quinoa.
- 25% of a cup of chopped fresh cilantro
- Salt and pepper

Instructions:
1. The quinoa and 2 cups of water should be put in a medium saucepan. When the quinoa is tender and the water has been absorbed, simmer for 15 to 20

minutes after bringing it to a boil over medium-high heat.

2. Make a big skillet hot over medium-high heat while the quinoa is cooking. Black beans should be added and heated thoroughly for 5-7 minutes.

3. Four bowls will each receive some cooked quinoa and black beans. Avocado slices, salsa, and cilantro are sprinkled on top of each bowl. According to taste, add salt and pepper.

Brown Rice And Grilled Vegetable And Shrimp Kebabs

This is a tasty and nutritious dinner option is grilled shrimp and vegetable kebabs. In this dish, shrimp that is high in protein is grilled to perfection on skewers with colorful vegetables that are also packed with nutrients. It makes a full and satisfying meal when placed over a bed of brown rice.

Ingredients:
- Peeled and deveined 1 pound of shrimp
- Slice of one zucchini
- A single chopped red bell pepper
- A single minced red onion
- One-half cup of cherry tomatoes
- 2 tablespoons olive oil

- 1 teaspoon of honey
- Garlic, minced from 2 cloves
- 1 tablespoon of smoked paprika
- Salt and pepper.
- Skewers made of metal or wood
- Cooked brown rice in two cups

Instructions:
1. Turn on the medium-high heat on your grill. For at least 30 minutes, soak wooden skewers in water if you're using them to avoid burning.

2. Mix the honey, olive oil, smoked paprika, minced garlic, salt, and pepper in a small bowl. Dispose of.

3. Shrimp and vegetables should be threaded onto skewers in a counter-clockwise direction.

4. The marinade is ready; just brush it on the skewers.

5. The skewers should be cooked for 3 to 4 minutes on each side, or until the vegetables are slightly charred and tender and the shrimp are pink and cooked through.

6. The skewers should be taken off the grill and left to cool down.

7. Brown rice should be placed on top of the shrimp and vegetable kebabs.

Hummus Wrap With Roasted Vegetables

If you're looking for a meatless lunch option, try the roasted vegetable and hummus wrap, which is a delicious and healthy choice. The wrap is a flavorful and filling option because it is bursting with vitamins and nutrients. To make a roasted vegetable and hummus wrap, follow these steps:

Ingredients:
- 1 whole grain wrap
- 1/8 cup of hummus
- 1/2 cup of roasted vegetables in various combinations (such as zucchini, eggplant, red peppers, and onions)
- Feta cheese, chopped into 1/4 cup
- Tiny spinach leaves in a handful
- Salt and pepper.

Instructions:

1. Set the oven's temperature to 400 °F. Olive oil, salt, and pepper, along with the vegetables' bite-sized pieces, are all that is needed to finish. They should be spread out on a baking sheet and baked for 20 to

25 minutes, or until they are tender and have a light browning.

2. The wrap can be warmed for a short while in the microwave or for about 30 seconds on each side in a dry skillet over medium heat.

3. A 1-inch border should be left around the edges of the wrap after spreading the hummus evenly over it.

4. Top the hummus with the roasted vegetables.

5. On top of the vegetables, scatter the feta cheese crumbles.

6. The feta cheese should be topped with a few baby spinach leaves.

7. Tucking in the sides as you roll the wrap tightly.

8. To serve right away, split the wrap in half.

Grilled Chicken And Steamed Vegetables In a Bowl Of Brown Rice

A healthy and satisfying meal that is ideal for lunch or dinner is a bowl of brown rice topped with grilled chicken and steamed vegetables. This meal is a great option for anyone looking for a balanced and nutritious meal because it is high in protein, fiber, and important vitamins and minerals.

Served over a bed of brown rice, this dish combines grilled chicken with steamed vegetables. A delicious and filling meal that will leave you satisfied and energized is created by the blending of flavors and textures. The following procedures to prepare a brown rice bowl with grilled chicken and steamed vegetables:

Ingredients:
- One cup of brown rice
- Two cups of water
- Two chicken breasts.
- One tablespoon of olive oil
- Salt and pepper
- 2 cups of mixed vegetables (such as broccoli, carrots, and bell peppers)

Instructions:

1. Put the brown rice in a medium saucepan after thoroughly rinsing it in a fine-mesh strainer. Bring to a boil over high heat while adding two cups of water.

2. Rice should be simmered, and covered, for 40 to 45 minutes, or until it is tender and the water has been absorbed. Reduce the heat to low.

3. Medium-high heat should be set on the grill.

4. Olive oil and salt and pepper should be applied to the chicken breasts.

5. The chicken should be cooked through after grilling for 6 to 8 minutes on each side.

6. Vegetable preparation can be done while the chicken is grilling. The vegetables should be cooked in the steamer until they are crisp but still tender.

7. Let the chicken rest after it has finished cooking completely before slicing it into strips.

8. Divide the brown rice among the four bowls to be used for assembly. Chicken slices and steamed vegetables should be placed on top of each bowl.

To suit your preferences, this recipe can be altered by substituting other vegetables, such as mushrooms, zucchini, or squash, as well as different seasoning blends. To intensify the flavors even further, you can also add a dressing or sauce, like a balsamic vinaigrette or a peanut sauce.

Grilled Chicken And Quinoa With a Greek Salad

Fresh vegetables, lean protein, and beneficial whole grains all come together in this delicious Greek salad with grilled chicken and quinoa. It takes only a few minutes to prepare and is a simple and wholesome meal.

Ingredients:

- Chicken breasts, grilled and sliced, weighing one pound.
- Four cups of mixed greens
- 1 cup of halved cherry tomatoes
- 1 cup of sliced red onion
- 1 cucumber
- Olives, half a cup, kalamata
- Feta cheese, broken up into 1/2 cup.
- 0.5 cups of cooked quinoa
- Extra virgin olive oil, one-fourth cup
- Red wine vinegar, 2 tablespoons.
- 1 minced clove of garlic
- Oregano, dry, 1 teaspoon
- Salt and pepper.

Instructions:

1. Follow the directions on the quinoa package to cook it, then set it aside.
2. Sliced cherry tomatoes, halved cucumber, red onion, feta cheese, kalamata olives, and mixed greens should all be combined in a large bowl.
3. Extra-virgin olive oil, red wine vinegar, chopped garlic, dried oregano, salt, and pepper should all be combined in a small bowl.
4. Mix the salad by adding the dressing and drizzling it over it.

5. Prepared quinoa and sliced, grilled chicken are added to the salad after it has been divided into bowls.

Greens And Turkey Chili

This meal is ideal for lunch or dinner, the mixed greens add a crisp, reviving flavor and are high in fiber and protein.

Ingredients:
- A pound of ground turkey
- 1 diced onion
- 2 minced garlic cloves
- 1 diced each of the red, green, and jalapeo peppers
- 1 diced each of the jalapeo peppers
- 1 can (14.5 oz) tomatoes in dice
- kidney beans from a single, rinsed, 15-ounce can.
- Black beans, 1 can (15 oz.), rinsed and drained
- 1 tablespoon chili powder
- Ground cumin, 1 teaspoon
- 1/2 teaspoon smoked paprika
- Salt and pepper.
- Greens mixture

Instructions:

1. Cook ground turkey until browned over medium-high heat in a big pot or Dutch oven,

breaking up the meat as it cooks with a wooden spoon.

2. Vegetables should be soft after 5-7 minutes of cooking when you add the onion, garlic, red, green, and jalapeo peppers to the pot.
3. Chili powder, ground cumin, smoked paprika, salt, and pepper should all be added to the pot along with diced tomatoes (and any juices they may contain).
4. To thicken the chili and combine the flavors, bring it to a simmer and cook it for 15 to 20 minutes.
5. Over a mixture of greens, serve the chili.

Salsa, Black Beans, And Baked Sweet Potatoes

The grilled vegetable and hummus sandwich on whole grain bread and the baked sweet potato with black beans and salsa are both healthy and satisfying meals that can be eaten for lunch or dinner. While black beans serve as a good source of protein and fiber, sweet potatoes are high in fiber, vitamins, and minerals. Salsa gives the food more flavor and nutrition.

Ingredients:
- 1 large sweet potato
- A half-cup of black beans
- 2:1 salsa
- 1 tablespoon olive oil
- Salt and pepper.

Instructions:

1. Set the oven's temperature to 400 °F (205 °C).
2. After cleaning, poke the sweet potato with a fork all over.
3. Olive oil, salt, and pepper are applied after rubbing the sweet potato.
4. Bake the sweet potato for 40–45 minutes, or until it is tender and easily pierced with a fork, on a baking sheet.
5. Black beans should be warmed through in a small pan over medium heat while you wait.
6. Slice open the cooked sweet potato after it has finished cooking, then top with black beans.
7. Black beans with salsa on top

Sandwich On Whole Grain Bread With Grilled Vegetables And Hummus

The grilled vegetable and hummus sandwich is an appetizing and nutritious choice, with the grilled vegetables adding a variety of vitamins and minerals and the hummus adding protein and fiber. This meal is satisfying and nutritious because whole-grain bread offers complex carbohydrates, fiber, and nutrients.

Ingredients:
- 2 pieces of whole-grain bread
- 2 tablespoons hummus

- A half-cup of grilled vegetables in various combinations (such as zucchini, bell peppers, and onions)
- Salt and pepper.

Instructions:

1. Heat a grill pan or the grill to a medium-high temperature.
2. Salt and pepper should be added after brushing the vegetables with olive oil.
3. The vegetables should be grilled for 5–6 minutes, or until they are soft and just beginning to char.
4. Bread should be lightly golden while toasted.
5. Both slices of bread should be covered with hummus.
6. The grilled vegetables should be arranged on one slice of bread.
7. Sandwich it together with the remaining slice of bread.
8. Along with the black beans and baked sweet potato, cut the sandwich in half and serve.

Brown Rice And Tofu In a Vegetable Stir-Fry

An incredibly flavorful and nutrient-dense vegetarian supper, this stir-fried vegetable dish with tofu, brown rice, and vegetables is also healthful. For a tasty and full dinner, marinated tofu is stir-fried with vibrant veggies that have been mildly spiced. This stir-fry will quickly become a household favorite when it is served over a bed of fluffy brown rice.

Ingredients:
- One cup of brown rice, uncooked
- 1 firm tofu block, pressed, then cut into cubes
- 2 cloves of minced garlic
- 1 red bell pepper
- 1 yellow bell pepper
- 1 onion
- 1 red bell pepper, sliced
- 10 ounces of broccoli florets
- Slicing up a cup of mushrooms
- A tbsp. of sesame oil
- 2 teaspoons of soy sauce
- Two teaspoons of rice vinegar
- 10 grams of honey
- 1/9 cup cornstarch
- Two teaspoons of water
- Salt and pepper
- Thinly sliced green onions (for garnish)

Instructions:

1. As directed on the packaging, prepare brown rice.

2. Sesame oil, soy sauce, rice vinegar, honey, cornstarch, and water should all be combined in a small basin to form a marinade.

3. Cubed tofu should be placed in the marinade and gently coated. A minimum of 10 minutes should pass so it can marinate.

4. Some oil should be heated over high heat in a big wok or pan. When aromatic, stir-fry the chopped onions and garlic for one to two minutes after adding them.

5. After adding the mushrooms, broccoli florets, and sliced bell peppers, stir-fry the ingredients for 2 to 3 minutes, or until the veggies are just starting to soften.

6. Tofu will be thoroughly cooked after being added to the wok and stir-fried for an additional two to three minutes.

7. According to taste, add salt and pepper.

8. On a bed of cooked brown rice, serve the stir-fry.

9. Cut up some green onions for the garnish.

Granola With a Low Glycemic Index And Greek Yogurt

Healthy and tasty options for breakfast or a snack include Greek yogurt with mixed berries and low-GI granola. Greek yogurt is a great source of probiotics, calcium, and protein, all of which are crucial for intestinal health. Mixed berries bring sweetness and antioxidants naturally, while low-GI granola offers complex carbs for long-lasting energy. You may add your preferred fruit and granola to this dish, which is simple to make.

Ingredients:
- 1 cup of unflavored Greek yogurt
- 1/2 cup of mixed berries (such as strawberries, blueberries, and raspberries)
- 1/4 cup low-GI granola

Instructions:

1. Greek yogurt that is plain, 1 cup, should be put in a bowl.
2. In the dish containing the yogurt, place 1/2 cup of chopped, rinsed mixed berries.
3. On top of the yogurt and berries, mix in 1/4 cup of low-GI granola.

Notes: This recipe works with either fresh or frozen berries. Try to find whole grain, nut, and seed-based low-GI granola. Sprinkle a little honey on top of the yogurt and berries for an extra delicious touch.

Feta Cheese With a Salad Of Roasted Vegetables And Quinoa
It is a well-balanced meal that will keep you feeling satiated for hours since it is loaded with wholesome veggies, protein-rich quinoa, and tangy feta cheese.

Ingredients:
- Quinoa, one cup
- Water in 2 cups
- 2 cups of various veggies (such as bell peppers, zucchini, onions, and carrots)
- 1 teaspoon of olive oil
- Salt and pepper
- A quarter cup of feta cheese crumbles

Instructions:

1. Your oven should be preheated at 400°F (200°C).

2. Before adding it to a medium-sized saucepan, the quinoa must be properly rinsed in a fine-mesh strainer. Bring to a boil over high heat while adding the water and a dash of salt.

3. Quinoa should simmer for approximately 15 minutes, or until all the water has been absorbed, on low heat with the lid on the pot. After turning off the heat, leave the covered pot stand for five minutes.

4. Cut the veggies into bite-sized pieces and combine them with the olive oil, salt, and pepper in a big bowl while the quinoa is cooking.

5. The veggies should be spread out on a baking sheet and roasted for 20 to 25 minutes, or until they are soft and have developed a light browning.

6. Just after the quinoa and veggies have finished cooking, let them cool.

7. Roasted veggies and quinoa should be combined in a large mixing basin. Combine everything and then sprinkle on the feta cheese.

8. At room temperature or heated, serve the salad. Also, you may keep any leftovers for up to three days in the refrigerator.

The Combination Of Whole Grain Crackers With Chicken And Vegetable Soup

Lunch or supper can be served with chicken and vegetable soup, which is a hearty and filling dish. This dish is a good choice for every day of the week since it's loaded with healthful components including chicken, veggies, and whole-grain crackers.

Ingredients:
- One tablespoon of olive oil
- Chopped one onion
- Garlic, minced from two cloves
- Peeling and chopping two carrots
- 4 cups of low-sodium chicken broth
- 2 celery stalks, diced
- 1 cup of cooked and chopped chicken breast
- Diced tomatoes in one can
- 2 teaspoons of dried thyme
- Salt and pepper.
- Granola crackers

Instructions:

1. In a big saucepan over medium heat, warm up the olive oil. Cook for about 5 minutes, until the onion and garlic are tenders.

2. Cook for a further 5 minutes after adding the celery and carrots to the saucepan.

3. Boiling will ensue after adding the chicken broth.

4. Add salt, pepper, dried thyme, and chopped tomatoes, and turn the heat to low. Shredded chicken is then added.

5. Once the veggies are cooked through, simmer for 20 to 25 minutes.

6. Hot servings should be accompanied by whole-grain crackers.

7. Enjoy your nourishing and tasty chicken and vegetable soup with whole-grain crackers!

Avo-Topped Tacos With Black Beans, And Sweet Potatoes

Vegetarian tacos made with black beans, sweet potatoes, and avocado are a tasty and nutritious midweek supper option. Besides being filling, the combination of sweet potatoes, black beans, and avocado is also rich in nutrients. Making it is as follows:

Ingredients:

- Peeled and chopped two big sweet potatoes
- Draining and rinsing one can of black beans
- Sliced avocado
- 1/2 red onion
- 1 bell pepper
- 2 minced garlic cloves.
- 1 tablespoon of chili powder
- 1 tablespoon cumin
- 1/3 tsp. paprika
- Salt and pepper
- Eight corn tortillas
- For garnish: cilantro
- For serving: lime wedges

Instructions:

1. Set the oven's temperature to 400 °F.
2. Sprinkle the diced sweet potatoes with salt, pepper, cumin, chili powder, and 1 tablespoon of olive oil in a large bowl.
3. On a baking sheet, spread the sweet potatoes out in a single layer and roast for 20 to 25 minutes, or until they are soft and just beginning to become crispy.
4. At this time, a big skillet with medium heat should be filled with one tablespoon of olive oil. For 5-7

minutes, or until the veggies are soft, add the diced red onion and bell pepper.

5. Stir till cooked through after adding the black beans and minced garlic to the pan.

6. In a pan or oven, reheat the corn tortillas.

7. Place a tablespoon of the black bean mixture, some roasted sweet potatoes, avocado slices, and another scoop on each tortilla before assembling the tacos. Include lime wedges with the garnish of cilantro.

Cooked Chicken With Whole Grain Croutons, Make a Caesar Salad

Cooked chicken For lunch or dinner, a delicious and healthy meal like a Caesar salad with whole grain croutons is a great option. The whole grain croutons give the salad a satisfying crunch, and it is a light, refreshing dish that is stuffed with protein and fiber. The Caesar dressing is a lighter and healthier alternative because it is made with Greek yogurt rather than mayonnaise. You can adjust this salad to your tastes and make it quickly.

Ingredients:
- 2 chicken breasts without the bones or the skin.
- A washed and chopped head of romaine lettuce
- Grated parmesan cheese in a quarter cup
- 1/2 cup of croutons made of whole grains
- One-fourth cup of plain Greek yogurt

- 1 teaspoon Dijon mustard
- Freshly squeezed lemon juice, 1 tablespoon
- Garlic clove, minced, one
- Salt and pepper

Instructions:

1. Grill should be preheated to medium-high.

2. Sprinkle salt and pepper on both sides of the chicken breasts.

3. The chicken should be grilled for 5 to 6 minutes on each side, or until it reaches an internal temperature of 165°F.

4. Before slicing it into thin strips, let the chicken rest for a few minutes.

5. The Greek yogurt, Dijon mustard, lemon juice, garlic, salt, and pepper should all be incorporated into a small bowl to form the Caesar dressing.

6. The romaine lettuce has been chopped, the chicken has been sliced, and the parmesan cheese has been grated.

7.   Add the Caesar dressing to the salad and toss to combine.

8.   Use the whole grain croutons to garnish the salad.

With Mixed Greens, a Spinach And Feta Frittata

This protein- and nutrient-rich frittata with spinach and feta is a delicious and healthy option for breakfast or brunch. The mixed greens add freshness and a pleasant crunch, and the flavorful combination of feta and spinach makes it taste delicious. A low-carb or gluten-free diet enthusiast will also enjoy this dish.

Ingredients:
● Six eggs, large
● 20 ounces of chopped fresh spinach
● Feta cheese, broken up into 1/2 cup.
● 1/4 cup minced onion
● Single minced garlic clove
● 1 tablespoon olive oil
● Salt and pepper
● Greens mixture

Instructions:

1.   The oven should be heated to 375°F (190°C).

2. Eggs, salt, and pepper should be combined in a sizable bowl.
3. A 10-inch oven-safe skillet with medium heat is where the olive oil is heated. The onion should be translucent when you add the chopped onion and minced garlic.
4. Sweat the spinach until wilted, 2 to 3 minutes, then add the spinach, chopped.
5. The spinach and onions in the skillet will receive the egg mixture on top. The feta cheese crumbles should be distributed on top.
6. Bake the frittata for 12 to 15 minutes, or until it is set and the top is browned, in the preheated oven after transferring the skillet.
7. Once out of the oven, take the skillet out and give it some time to cool.
8. A side of mixed greens should be served with the frittata after cutting it into wedges.

Stir-Fry With Brown Rice And Lentils And Vegetables

Veggies will love the flavorful and nutritious stir-fry with lentils. Lentils, brown rice, and colorful vegetables are great sources of fiber and protein, as well as vitamins and other nutrients. Perfect for a weeknight dinner, this recipe comes together quickly.

Ingredients:

- One cup of brown rice
- Two cups of water
- 1 tablespoon olive oil
- Red and yellow bell peppers
- An onion
- Two cloves of minced garlic
- Two cups of broccoli florets
- A cup of sliced mushrooms
- Lentils from one can rinsed and drained.
- 2 tablespoons of soy sauce
- 1 tablespoon of honey
- 1 tablespoon of sesame oil
- 1/2 teaspoon of red pepper flakes
- Salt and pepper.

Instructions:

1. Put the brown rice in a pot with 2 cups of water after giving it a thorough rinse in a strainer with fine mesh. It should be heated to a rolling boil before being simmered for 45 minutes on low heat with the lid on the pot.

2. A big skillet with medium heat should be used to warm the olive oil. For about two to three minutes, add the onion and garlic and cook until soft.

3. To the skillet, add the florets from the broccoli, red and yellow bell peppers, and thinly sliced mushrooms. When the vegetables are crisp-tender, cook for 5-7 minutes.

4. In the skillet with the vegetables, add the lentils that have been rinsed and drained, and stir to incorporate.

5. Put the soy sauce, honey, sesame oil, and red pepper flakes in a small bowl and whisk to combine. Then, after adding the sauce, stir everything together to ensure that it is all evenly coated. Until heated all the way through, cook for an additional 2-3 minutes.

6. Over a bed of brown rice, plate the stir-fry with the vegetables and lentils. to taste, incorporate salt and pepper.

With Mixed Greens,A Turkey, And An Avocado Wrap

For a quick and simple lunch that is also filling and healthy, try a turkey and avocado wrap with mixed greens. This is a well-balanced meal because it combines fiber from the greens with protein from the turkey and good fats from the avocado.

Ingredients:

- A single whole-wheat tortilla
- Several slices of turkey breast
- Avocado, cut in half.
- 1/4 cup of mixed greens
- a quarter cup of grated carrots
- 1 teaspoon hummus

Instructions:

1. On a plate or cutting board, spread out the tortilla evenly.
2. The tortilla should be covered in hummus evenly.
3. The hummus is followed by layers of turkey, avocado, mixed greens, and shredded carrots.
4. Tucking the ends in as you roll the tortilla tightly.
5. Sharpen your knife and split the wrap in half.
6. If you want to take it with you, wrap it in foil or plastic wrap before serving.
7. The ingredients in this wrap can be changed to suit your tastes if you so choose. Alternate tortillas can be used, and you can substitute grilled chicken or tofu for the turkey as a source of protein.

Goat Cheese And A Walnut-Topped Salad Of Roasted Beets

A delicious and healthy salad that is ideal for lunch or dinner is the one with roasted beets, goat cheese, and walnuts. For anyone looking to improve their diet, this salad is a fantastic option because it is full of nutrients and antioxidants. A tasty and filling meal is created by combining roasted beets with creamy goat cheese and crunchy walnuts.

Ingredients:

- Three small beets, peeled and chopped
- Two tablespoons of olive oil
- Salt and pepper.
- Four cups of mixed greens
- A half-cup of goat cheese crumbles
- A half cup of chopped walnuts
- Two tablespoons of balsamic vinegar
- 10 grams of honey
- 1/4 cup of olive oil

Instructions:

1. Set the oven's temperature to 400 °F.
2. Then, add 2 tablespoons of olive oil, salt, and pepper to the bowl with the chopped beets.
3. Beets should be baked for 25 to 30 minutes, or until tender, in a single layer on a baking sheet.
4. Dressing preparation can be done while the beets are roasting. Balsamic vinegar, honey, and 1/4 cup of olive oil should be mixed together in a small bowl. Dispose of.

5. The beets should be taken out of the oven once they have finished roasting and should be given some time to cool.
6. Put the roasted beets, mixed greens, goat cheese crumbles, and walnuts in a big bowl.
7. Mix the salad by adding the dressing and drizzling it over it.

Hummus On a Wrap With Grilled Chicken And Vegetables

A quick and nutritious lunch or dinner can be made using this recipe. This hearty and flavorful dish is made up of grilled chicken, mixed vegetables, and whole wheat tortillas.

Ingredients:
- 2 chicken breasts without the bones or the skin.
- Sliced red and yellow bell peppers
- Zucchini
- Half a Red onion
- 2 tablespoons of olive oil.
- Salt and pepper
- 4 whole-wheat tortillas
- 1/2 cup hummus

Instructions:

1. The heat should be set to medium-high on the grill or grill pan.
2. Add salt and pepper and drizzle olive oil over the chicken breasts, bell peppers, zucchini, and red onion.
3. Grill the chicken for 6 to 8 minutes on each side, or until it reaches a temperature of 165°F inside.
4. Place the sliced vegetables on the grill and cook for 4-6 minutes per side, or until fork-tender and slightly charred.
5. When finished grilling, take the chicken and vegetables off and set them aside to cool.
6. Set aside the chicken breasts after slicing them into thin strips.
7. A tablespoon of hummus should be spread on each tortilla before assembling the wraps.
8. The tortillas should each have a portion of the grilled vegetables and chicken strips.
9. Tuck the ends inside as you roll the tortillas tightly.
10. Serve the wraps right away or chill until ready to eat by wrapping them tightly in plastic wrap.

Brown Rice And a Curry Made Of Chickpeas And Vegetables

An excellent vegetarian dish for a filling lunch or dinner is chickpea and vegetable curry. It is both healthy and delicious. This curry is satiating and nourishing, being loaded with protein, fiber, and important nutrients. By including brown rice, which offers complex carbohydrates for enduring energy, it becomes a complete meal. To prepare this delectable and simple recipe, follow these steps:

Ingredients:

- Drained and washed chickpeas from one can
- One red bell pepper
- One green bell pepper
- One zucchini
- One can of diced tomatoes
- One onion, chopped
- Two cloves of garlic, minced
- 1 teaspoon curry powder
- 1 tablespoon cumin
- 1 teaspoon of coriander
- 1/2 teaspoon turmeric
- 1/8 tsp cayenne pepper
- One cup of vegetable broth
- Salt and pepper.
- 1/2 cup cooked brown rice

Instructions:

1. Medium-high heat should be used to warm a sizable skillet. For 1-2 minutes, or until the onion is translucent, add the onion and garlic.

2. Sliced peppers and zucchini should be added to the skillet and cooked for an additional 5-7 minutes, or until soft.

3. Curry powder, cumin, coriander, turmeric, and cayenne pepper should all be added to the skillet along with the chickpeas and diced tomatoes. Combined by stirring.

4. Bring the mixture to a simmer after adding the vegetable broth to the skillet. The flavors should have merged by the time the curry has simmered for 10 to 15 minutes.

5. Add pepper and salt to taste when preparing the curry.

6. On top of cooked brown rice, dish up the chickpea and vegetable curry.

For meal prepping or feeding a large group, this recipe yields 4-6 servings. For those with dietary restrictions, it is a fantastic option because it is also vegan and gluten-free.

A tahini-Dressed Bowl Of Quinoa And Roasted Vegetables

It's simple to make a filling and healthy meal with this quinoa and roasted vegetable bowl with tahini dressing. Being both gluten-free and vegan, it's a fantastic option for lunch or dinner. A healthy source of fiber and protein is provided by roasted vegetables and quinoa, and a rich and nutty flavor is added by the tahini dressing.

Ingredients:
- A cup of quinoa
- Two cups of water
- 2 cups of mixed vegetables (such as broccoli, carrots, and bell peppers)
- One tablespoon of olive oil
- Salt and pepper.
- 1/4 cup tahini
- 1 teaspoon lemon juice
- 2 teaspoons of water
- 1 minced clove of garlic

Instructions:

1. Set the oven's temperature to 400 °F (200 °C).
2. In a pot, combine the rinsed quinoa with two cups of water. To cook the quinoa and allow the water to be

absorbed, bring it to a boil, then lower the heat to a simmer for 15 to 20 minutes.

3. The mixed vegetables should be chopped into bite-sized pieces while the quinoa is cooking.
4. Olive oil and salt and pepper to taste should be added before tossing the vegetables.
5. On a baking sheet, arrange the vegetables in a single layer and roast them for 15 to 20 minutes, or until they are tender and have developed a light browning.
6. Tahini, lemon juice, water, and minced garlic are combined to make the dressing in a small bowl.
7. Divide the cooked quinoa between two bowls, then top each bowl with some roasted vegetables. Serve the dish after adding tahini dressing.

Whole Grain Bread, A Tomato And Mozzarella Salad

An age-old summertime dish that is both reviving and filling is tomato and mozzarella salad. For added texture and fiber, this recipe includes whole-grain bread in the mix. This delicious and healthy option is excellent for lunch or a light dinner.

Ingredients:
*   2-4 mature tomatoes
*   A pound of fresh mozzarella cheese
*   Two to three tablespoons of extra virgin olive oil

- A couple of tablespoons of balsamic vinegar
- Salt and pepper.
- Fresh basil leaves, about ten of them
- 2 pieces of whole-grain bread

Instructions:

1. The tomatoes and mozzarella should first be cut into 1/4-inch-thick slices. Alternately place each of them in a bowl or serving plate.
2. Combine the olive oil and balsamic vinegar in a small bowl by whisking them together thoroughly. The tomato and mozzarella slices should be covered with the mixture.
3. Taste-testing pepper and salt after sprinkling.
4. Sprinkle the salad with basil leaves that have been torn into small pieces.
5. Cut the whole grain bread slices into small pieces after toasting. The bread slices should be arranged around the bowl or serving dish's perimeter.

To give the salad even more flavor, you could also add some finely chopped red onion or garlic. A flavor-infused vinegar or olive oil can also be used to add some variety.

30 Recipes For Dinner

Fish Baked With Roast Veggies

An effortless, wholesome dish to make is baked salmon with roasted veggies. In contrast to roasted veggies, which offer a variety of vitamins and minerals, salmon is strong in protein and omega-3 fatty acids. Also, you may add your own veggies or seasonings to this recipe, making it incredibly adaptable.

Ingredients:
- Four salmon fillets
- Veggies, chopped into two cups (such as broccoli, bell peppers, and zucchini)
- 2 tablespoons olive oil
- Salt and pepper.
- Slices of lemon (optional)

Instructions:
1. Set the oven's temperature to 400 °F (200 °C).
2. Put parchment paper on a baking pan.
3. Dry the salmon fillets with paper towels after rinsing them.
4. Apply salt and pepper to taste the salmon fillets.
5. The skin-side-down salmon fillets should be placed on the baking sheet.

6. Olive oil, chopped veggies, salt, and pepper should all be combined in a bowl.
7. The salmon fillets on the baking pan are surrounded by the vegetable mixture.
8. Bake the salmon and veggies for 15 to 20 minutes, or until they are both cooked through.
9. With lemon wedges, if preferred, serve the fish and veggies.

Optional: To give the meal more flavor, you may also stir in other herbs or spices with the vegetable combination, like paprika, dried basil, or garlic powder. For a filling and healthful meal, this recipe is a fantastic choice. It may be tailored to incorporate your preferred veggies or spices and is simple to cook.

Peppers Filled With Quinoa

Veggies may enjoy this filling, flavorful, and nutritious dish made with quinoa-stuffed bell peppers. Bell peppers are used in this recipe, which is roasted to perfection after being packed with quinoa, veggies, and spices. Making it is as follows:

Ingredients:
*   3 peppers,
*   Uncooked 1 cup of quinoa
*   2.1 cups veggie broth

- 0.1 tsp. olive oil
- 2 cloves of garlic, minced
- 1 chopped onion
- 1 cup of chopped mushrooms
- 1 zucchini
- 1 yellow squash,
- 1 cup drained chopped tomatoes from one can (15 ounces).
- A tsp. of dried oregano
- One teaspoon of dried basil
- Salt and pepper.
- One cup of grated mozzarella cheese (optional)

Instructions:

1. Set the oven to 375 degrees Fahrenheit.

2. Remove the seeds and membranes from the bell peppers by cutting off their tops. peppers aside for now.

3. The quinoa and vegetable broth should be heated up in a big pot. To cook the quinoa and allow the stock to be fully absorbed, lower the heat, cover the pan, and simmer for about 20 minutes.

4. A big pan over medium-high heat should be heating the olive oil in the meantime. As soon as the onion

is transparent, add the garlic and onion and simmer for an additional 2–3 minutes.

5. For a further 5-7 minutes, or until the veggies are soft, add the mushrooms, zucchini, and yellow squash to the skillet.

6. Oregano, basil, salt, and pepper, along with the chopped tomatoes, are all added. Next, stir the cooked quinoa into the mixture in the pan.

7. Place the quinoa and veggie mixture into the bell peppers before placing them in a baking dish.

8. On top of each pepper, if preferred, grate some mozzarella cheese.

9. For 30-35 minutes, or until the peppers are soft and the cheese has melted, bake the dish with the foil cover on.

10. Bell peppers that have been stuffed should be served hot.

11. To accommodate your preferences or dietary constraints, this recipe is easily modifiable. To develop a distinctive taste profile, try substituting other veggies or putting in extra spices. Moreover,

you may omit the cheese or use a non-dairy cheese if you're vegan or lactose sensitive.

Baked Sweet Potatoes With Grilled Chicken

Roasted sweet potatoes and grilled chicken are two delicious and nutritious ingredients that go together beautifully in this meal. The chicken is marinated in a straightforward mixture of olive oil, lemon juice, garlic, and herbs for flavoring, and the sweet potatoes are seasoned with a combination of spices for a delectable and wholesome side dish.

Ingredients:
- Boneless, skinless chicken breasts, two
- Two medium-sized sweet potatoes, chopped and peeled
- Two teaspoons of olive oil
- Juice of one tablespoon of lemon
- Garlic, minced from two cloves
- A tsp. of dried oregano
- 1/4 teaspoon salt
- 1/8 tsp. black pepper
- A half-teaspoon of paprika
- 1/4 teaspoon cumin

Instructions:

1. On a baking sheet, spread parchment paper and preheat the oven to 400°F (200°C).

2. Mix the olive oil, lemon juice, garlic, dried oregano, salt, and pepper in a small bowl.

3. The marinade should be poured over the chicken breasts after placing them in a large resealable plastic bag. Affirming that the chicken is equally coated, seal the bag and massage any remaining marinade into the meat. At least 30 minutes should pass while the chicken is marinating in the fridge.

4. Diced sweet potatoes are mixed with paprika, cumin, and a little salt in a mixing basin while this is going on.

5. In the preheated oven, roast the seasoned sweet potatoes for 20 to 25 minutes, or until they are soft and lightly browned, flipping halfway through cooking.

6. Using a medium-high heat source, preheat a grill pan. Add the chicken breasts that have been marinating, then grill for approximately 6-7 minutes on each side, or until the chicken is cooked through and the middle is no longer pink.

7. Before slicing the chicken into strips, allow it to rest for 5 minutes.

8. With optional green onions or chopped fresh herbs as a garnish, serve the grilled chicken alongside the roasted sweet potatoes.

Bread Made With Nutritious Grains And Lentil Soup

An excellent meal for chilly days is lentil soup, which is hearty, reassuring, and nourishing. As a nutritious and satiating component of any soup, lentils are a great source of protein, fiber, vitamins, and minerals. Whole grain bread, a wonderful source of complex carbs, fiber, and minerals, is served as a side dish with this meal.

Ingredients:
- 1 cup of dry lentils, drained and rinsed.
- 2 carrots, diced;
- 2 stalks of celery, diced
- 1 onion, chopped;
- 3 garlic cloves, minced
- Diced tomatoes in one can
- Six cups of veggie broth and one bay leaf
- 1/tsp dried thyme
- Salt and pepper.
- Whole-grain bread

Instructions:

1. Over medium heat, warm up some oil in a big saucepan. The onions should be tender and transparent after 5 minutes of cooking after being added.

2. The saucepan should now contain the chopped celery, carrots, and garlic. Cook for a further five minutes after combining.

3. Stir together the lentils after draining and rinsing them.

4. Bay leaves, dried thyme, and chopped tomatoes are added after pouring in the vegetable broth. Combined by stirring.

5. The lentils should be ready after 30 to 40 minutes of simmering, so bring the soup to a boil before turning the heat down to a low setting.

6. Add salt and pepper to taste and discard the bay leaf from the soup.

7. Set your oven to 375°F (190°C) and simmer the soup while it is doing so. Place thick slices of whole-grain bread on a baking pan.

8. Once the bread is crispy and golden brown, bake it for 10 to 15 minutes.

9. As soon as the soup is finished cooking, spoon it into bowls and serve with the whole grain bread to the side.

Brown Rice, Tofu, And Stir-Fried Vegetables.

A tasty and nutritious supper that is simple to prepare is this stir-fry of tofu, vegetables, and brown rice. It is ideal for anybody who wants to have a balanced and full meal because it is packed with protein, fiber, and healthy fats. The meal may accommodate a variety of dietary requirements because it is also vegan and gluten-free.

Ingredients:
- Firm tofu in one block
- Cooked brown rice in two cups
- Sliced thinly, 1 red bell pepper
- Sliced thinly 1 yellow onion
- 2-cups worth of broccoli florets
- Minced two garlic cloves
- A teaspoon of grated ginger
- 2 teaspoons soy sauce
- 1 teaspoon hoisin sauce
- A single spoonful of sesame oil
- 2 teaspoons of vegetable oil

- Salt and pepper.

Instructions:

1. In order to eliminate any extra water, start by pressing the tofu. With a heavy item, such as a cast iron pan, on top, wrap the tofu with paper towels or a clean kitchen towel. Allowing it to drain should take 10 to 15 minutes.

2. Tofu is diced into small pieces and salt and pepper are added.

3. Large skillet set over medium-high heat to warm the vegetable oil. The tofu cubes should be added now and cooked for 3 to 4 minutes on each side, or until crispy and golden brown. Put aside after being removed from the skillet.

4. After adding the onions, sauté them in the skillet for two to three minutes, or until they start to soften. For a further 2 to 3 minutes, add the thinly sliced red bell pepper.

5. Next, swirl constantly for one minute while cooking the minced garlic and grated ginger in the pan.

6. For 5-7 minutes, or until they are crisp and tender, add the broccoli florets to the skillet.

7. To combine the soy sauce, hoisin sauce, and sesame oil, mix them all together in a small dish.

8. Pour the sauce over the fried tofu after placing it back in the skillet with the veggies. After the tofu and veggies are completely covered in sauce, everything has been well mixed.

9. A bed of cooked brown rice should be placed on top of the tofu and veggie stir fry.

Green Beans And Mushrooms

This hearty and filling dish is ideal for any season: mushroom risotto with green beans. The earthy flavor of mushrooms is infused into the creamy risotto, and the crisp, tender green beans are the ideal side dish. This dish is fantastic as a main course for vegetarians or as a tasty side dish to any meal.

Ingredients:
*   One cup of Arborio rice
*   4 cups vegetable stock
*   1 cup of sliced mushrooms
*   A single small onion, chopped finely

- Garlic, minced from two cloves
- 2 tablespoons of olive oil
- Half a cup of grated Parmesan cheese
- 1 tablespoon butter
- 1/8 cup dry white wine
- Black pepper and salt, as desired.
- Trimmed 1 lb of green beans

Instructions:

1. The vegetable broth should be heated slowly to a simmer in a big pot.

2. Heat the olive oil over medium-high heat in a separate, big saucepan. Stir in the minced garlic and onion, and cook for an additional two to three minutes, or until softened.

3. The onion, garlic, and arborio rice should all be combined before being added. When the rice is just beginning to toast, add another 2-3 minutes of sautéing.

4. Stirring is required to ensure complete absorption of the white wine after adding it to the rice mixture.

5. One cup at a time, start stirring the rice mixture with the hot vegetable broth, adding the next cup only

after the previous cup has been completely absorbed. Continue doing this until all the broth has been added and the rice is cooked all the way through.

6. A 400°F oven should be set up while the risotto is cooking. Sliced mushrooms should be spread out in a single layer on a baking sheet and roasted for 10 to 15 minutes, or until tender.

7. Remove the cooked risotto from the heat, then stir in the butter and Parmesan cheese. Depending on taste, season with salt and black pepper.

8. Steam the green beans for 3–4 minutes or until they are crisp–tender while the risotto is cooling.

9. Green beans and roasted mushrooms should be served alongside the mushroom risotto.

Zoodles And Baked Turkey Meatballs

Anyone looking to increase their intake of vegetables and lean protein in their diet will love the nutritious and delectable baked turkey meatballs with zucchini noodles. This meal has a lot of flavors and is low in carbohydrates and gluten. The zucchini noodles give traditional spaghetti a light and healthy twist, and the meatballs are juicy and tender thanks to a mixture of ground turkey, herbs, and spices. How to make baked turkey meatballs with zucchini noodles, step by step:

Ingredients:
- A pound of ground turkey
- 1 egg
- 1/4 cup of almond flour
- 2 tablespoons chopped fresh parsley
- 2 tablespoons freshly chopped basil
- 1/8 teaspoon of garlic powder
- 1/2 teaspoon of onion powder
- 1/2 teaspoon of salt
- 1/8 tsp. black pepper
- 4 medium zucchini
- 2 tablespoons of olive oil
- 2 cups of sauce for pasta

Instructions:

1. The oven should be heated to 375°F (190°C). Put parchment paper on a baking pan.

2. Mix the ground turkey, egg, almond flour, parsley, basil, garlic powder, onion powder, salt, and black pepper in a sizable bowl. The ingredients should be thoroughly combined and distributed throughout.

3. Place the meatballs made from the turkey mixture on the baking sheet that has been prepared.

4. Until the meatballs are cooked through and golden brown, bake them for 20 to 25 minutes.

5. Spiralize or peel zucchini to make noodles while the meatballs are baking. Use a vegetable peeler or a spiralizer to create thin strips of zucchini by cutting off the ends and spiralizing them. The zucchini noodles must be set aside.

6. In a sizable pan over medium heat, warm the olive oil. When the zucchini noodles are soft and lightly browned, add them and cook for an additional two to three minutes.

7. Zucchini noodles and marinara sauce should be combined thoroughly in a pan. Once the sauce is fully heated, cook for an additional 1–2 minutes.

8. Marinara sauce and zucchini noodles should be served with baked turkey meatballs on top.

Vegetable Kebabs And Grilled Shrimp

For a meal on a summer evening, try grilled shrimp and vegetable kebabs. In addition to being flavorful and simple to prepare, they are healthy. An eye-catching and delicious dish that is sure to impress your guests is created by grilling juicy shrimp with vibrant vegetables. This dish is suitable for a light main course or as a side dish to go with other grilled foods.

Ingredients:
- 1 pound of large, raw shrimp that have been peeled and deveined
- A single red bell pepper, chopped into pieces
- 1 yellow bell pepper, cut into pieces.
- 1 red onion cut into chunks
- One zucchini, chopped into pieces
- 1 teaspoon of olive oil
- Salt and pepper.
- Skewers made of metal or wood

Instructions:

1. To avoid them burning while grilling, give wooden skewers at least 30 minutes to soak in water.

2. Turn on the medium-high heat on your grill.

3. The skewers are threaded with a mixture of the following ingredients: shrimp, red bell pepper, yellow bell pepper, red onion, and zucchini.

4. Add salt and pepper and drizzle some olive oil over the skewers.

5. The vegetables and shrimp should be tender and slightly charred after cooking the skewers for two to three minutes on each side.

6. Before serving, take the skewers off the grill and give them a few seconds to cool.

7. With a hot side dish of your choice, such as brown rice or a green salad, serve the grilled shrimp and vegetable kebabs.

Root Vegetables & Slow-Cooked Beef Stew

It's a delicious and nourishing dish that's ideal for a cozy night in. Slow cooker beef stew with root vegetables. The slow cooker handles most of the work in making this dish, making it simple to prepare. A hearty and satisfying meal that the whole family will enjoy is made possible by tender beef and flavorful root vegetables.

Ingredients:
- Trimmed and diced into 1-inch cubes
- 2 pounds of beef chuck roast
- One tablespoon of olive oil
- Chopped one onion

- Minced four cloves of garlic
- 1.5 cups beef broth
- 1/2 cup of red wine
- Two tablespoons of tomato paste
- 2 teaspoons of dried thyme
- 1 tsp. dried rosemary
- One bay leaf
- Peeled and chopped into 1-inch pieces 3 carrots
- Peeled and cut into 1-inch pieces
- Three parsnips sliced into 1-inch pieces
- 2 turnips, peeled
- Salt and pepper

Instructions:

1. Melt the butter over medium-high heat in a large skillet. 5 minutes should be enough time to brown the beef after adding it.

2. To the slow cooker, add the beef.

3. In the same skillet, combine the onion and garlic. Cook, stirring occasionally, for about 3 minutes, or until soft.

4. Thyme, rosemary, bay leaf, tomato paste, red wine, and beef broth are all added to the skillet and combined.

5. The beef in the slow cooker should be covered with the mixture.

6. Stirring will help combine the turnips, parsnips, and carrots in the slow cooker.

7. According to taste, add salt and pepper.

8. When the beef and vegetables are tender, cook them covered in the slow cooker for 8–10 hours or on high for 4–6 hours.

9. Eliminate and discard the bay leaf.

10. With crusty bread or mashed potatoes, if preferred, serve the beef stew hot.

Roasted Carrots And Brussels Sprouts Served With Baked Chicken

It's simple to make a delicious and nutritious meal by baking chicken with roasted carrots and Brussels sprouts. The vegetables and chicken are baked together while the chicken is seasoned with herbs and spices. For the ideal side dish to go with the juicy chicken, roast the carrots and Brussels sprouts until they are soft and slightly caramelized. For a quick weeknight meal or meal preparation for the week, this dish is ideal.

Ingredients:
- Four skin-on, bone-in chicken thighs
- Four medium carrots; each peeled and finely chopped.
- Trimmed and cut in half 1 pound of Brussels sprouts
- Two teaspoons of olive oil
- 1 tsp. of garlic powder
- 2 teaspoons of dried thyme
- 1 tsp. dried rosemary
- One tablespoon paprika
- Salt and pepper

Instructions:

1. Set the oven's temperature to 400 °F (200 °C).

2. Combine the thyme, rosemary, paprika, salt, and pepper in a small bowl along with the garlic powder.

3. Then, evenly distribute the herb and spice mixture over the chicken thighs after placing them on a baking sheet.

4. Chop the carrots and Brussels sprouts, then toss with the salt, pepper, and olive oil in a big bowl.

5. Lay the chicken thighs out on the baking sheet, surrounded by the seasoned vegetables.

6. When the chicken is cooked through and the vegetables are soft and caramelized, bake in the preheated oven for 30 to 40 minutes.

7. Freshly roasted vegetables and baked chicken should be served.

Vegetarian Curry And Brown Rice

This savory, nutritious, quick-to-prepare recipe is great for a weeknight supper because it is made with vegetables. This recipe is a fantastic choice for a warm and soothing lunch since it is full of nutrient-dense veggies and warming spices. A fulfilling and complete dinner is created by serving it with brown rice, which also adds fiber and complex carbs to the dish.

Ingredients:
- 1 tbsp. of coconut oil
- Diced 1 onion
- Minced three cloves of garlic
- 1/4 cup grated ginger
- Curry powder, 1 tablespoon
- 1 tablespoon of ground turmeric
- 1/8 tsp. cumin powder

- 1/2 tsp. coriander powder
- One-fourth of a teaspoon of cayenne (optional)
- Peeled and chopped one sweet potato
- Sliced zucchini
- Chopped red bell pepper
- One 15-ounce can of washed and drained chickpeas.
- 1 can (14 ounces) (14 ounces) tomatoes in dice
- 50% of a cup of vegetable broth
- Salt and pepper.
- 1/2 cup cooked brown rice
- Fresh cilantro.

Instructions:

1. Set a large saucepan over medium heat to warm it up. onions are translucent after 5 minutes of sautéing with coconut oil, onions, garlic, and ginger.

2. Stir in the cayenne pepper (if using), curry powder, turmeric, cumin, coriander, and cumin.

3. Fill the saucepan with vegetable broth, sweet potato, zucchini, red bell pepper, chickpeas, and chopped tomatoes. Bring it to a boil while stirring everything together.

4. Simmer the sweet potatoes for 20 to 25 minutes, until they are fork-tender, on low heat with the lid on.

5. Using salt and pepper to taste, season the vegetable curry.

6. Garnish with fresh cilantro before serving the stew over brown rice. Enjoy!

Note: If you would like, you may also use other veggies in the curry, such as eggplant, cauliflower, and carrots. According to the veggies you use, adjust the cooking time appropriately.

Vegetables And Shrimp In a Cauliflower Rice Stir-Fry

A tasty and nutritious dish that is low in carbohydrates and gluten is stir-fried cauliflower rice with shrimp and veggies. Given that it has fewer calories, carbs, and other nutrients like fiber, vitamins, and minerals than ordinary rice, cauliflower rice is a fantastic alternative. Shrimp and a range of vibrant veggies are also included in this recipe, which results in a nutrient-rich dinner that is also savory and filling.

Ingredients:
- Peeled and deveined 1 lb. of shrimp

- 1 head of grated cauliflower, cut up like rice.
- Thin pieces of two bell peppers
- Diced 1 onion
- Garlic, minced from two cloves
- 10 ounces of broccoli florets
- One cup of snow peas
- 1 tablespoon coconut oil
- 2 tablespoons of soy sauce
- 1 tablespoon sesame oil
- 1 teaspoon of honey
- Salt and pepper
- Thinly sliced green onions.

Instructions:

1. Heat coconut oil to a medium-high temperature in a large skillet or wok.
2. For two to three minutes, add the onion and garlic and sauté until tender.
3. For 5-7 minutes, or until the veggies are tender-crisp, add the bell peppers, broccoli, and snow peas.
4. In the skillet with the other veggies, add the grated cauliflower and mix well to blend.
5. Sesame oil, honey, soy sauce, salt, and pepper should all be combined in a small bowl.
6. Cauliflower and other vegetables should be covered equally with the sauce after it has been added.

7. When pink and cooked through, add the shrimp to the pan and cook for 3–4 minutes.

8. Sliced green onions are used to decorate the hot cauliflower rice stir fry.

9. It takes only a few minutes to prepare and is a flavorful, nutrient-dense supper when you stir-fry shrimp and veggies with cauliflower rice. It's an excellent way to consume a wide array of vibrant veggies, and the shrimp provides a fantastic amount of lean protein. It is possible to add your preferred veggies and seasonings to this recipe, which is highly adaptable.

Spaghetti Squash With a Sauce Made Of Turkey Meat

As an excellent and low-carb substitute for classic spaghetti and meat sauce, try spaghetti squash with turkey meat sauce. When cooked, the nutritious vegetable spaghetti squash resembles spaghetti noodles in texture. Your need for a robust and filling lunch will be sated by this dish when served with a tasty turkey meat sauce.

The following items are needed to prepare spaghetti squash with turkey meat sauce:

- 1 spaghetti squash
- A pound of ground turkey

- One sliced tiny onion
- Garlic, minced from two cloves
- Tomatoes, diced, in a can (14 oz.)
- Tomato sauce from one (8-ounce) can
- Tomato paste, 1 tablespoon
- 1-tablespoon dried basil
- Oregano, dry, 1 teaspoon
- Salt and pepper
- Grated Parmesan cheese (optional)

The directions, in detail, are as follows:

1. Set the oven's temperature to 400 °F (200 °C).
2. In order to remove the seeds and pulp, cut the spaghetti squash in half lengthwise.
3. The squash should be baked for 30 to 40 minutes, depending on the size, or until a fork can easily pierce the flesh when placed cut-side down on a baking pan.
4. Make the beef sauce while the butternut squash is cooking. Once the meat is browned and the onions are soft, sauté the ground turkey, onion, and garlic in a large pan over medium heat.
5. Sprinkle salt, pepper, basil, oregano, tomato paste, tomato sauce, and chopped tomatoes over the skillet's contents. Once everything is mixed, boil the mixture.

6. The sauce should simmer for 15 to 20 minutes with occasional stirring after reducing the heat.
7. Remove the spaghetti squash from the oven after it is finished cooking and allow it to cool. For lengthy, spaghetti-like strands of squash flesh, use a fork to scrape it from the skin.
8. Spoon the turkey meat sauce over the spaghetti squash once you've divided it up into serving dishes. If preferred, top the food with freshly grated Parmesan.

With a Mixed Greens Salad, Bake Eggplant Parmesan

The traditional Italian meal may be transformed into a tasty and nutritious baked eggplant parmesan. It's an excellent method to increase the number of veggies in your diet, and the combination of tomato sauce, mozzarella cheese, and crispy eggplant makes for a filling dinner. This recipe is a healthful and substantial choice for lunch or supper when served with a mixed greens salad.

Ingredients:
- 2 medium eggplants, cut into rounds measuring 1/2 inch wide.
- 100 grams of whole wheat breadcrumbs
- Grated parmesan cheese, half a cup
- Two beaten eggs
- Two cups of tomato sauce

- One cup of grated mozzarella cheese
- Salt and pepper
- 2 tablespoons of olive oil
- 8 mugs of mixed greens
- Balsamic vinaigrette in a quarter cup

Instructions:

1. The oven should be heated to 375°F (190°C).
2. On a baking sheet, arrange the eggplant rounds and season with salt and pepper after brushing them with olive oil. Roast until fork-tender and golden brown for 20 to 25 minutes, turning once.
3. Parmesan cheese and breadcrumbs should be combined on a small plate. Eggs should be beaten in another shallow dish.
4. Each eggplant round should be dipped in the beaten eggs first, followed by the breadcrumb mixture, and any excess should be shaken off.
5. On a baking sheet that has been prepared, place the breaded eggplant rounds and bake for 15 to 20 minutes, or until crispy and golden brown.
6. Heat the tomato sauce to a warm consistency in a small saucepan over low heat.
7. Layer the tomato sauce, shredded mozzarella cheese, and rounds of roasted eggplant in a 9 x 13-inch baking dish. To finish, add a layer of mozzarella cheese on top after continuing the

layering process until all the ingredients have been utilized.

8. After the cheese is melted and bubbling, bake for 15-20 minutes.

9. The mixed greens salad may be made while the eggplant parmesan is baking. Mix the greens with the balsamic vinaigrette in a big basin.

10. A portion of mixed greens salad should be served alongside the hot baked eggplant parmesan.

Roasted Butternut Squash And Grilled Pork Tenderloin

Butternut squash and grilled pork tenderloin are tasty and nutritious dish that goes well with any meal or occasion. The roasted butternut squash's sweet and savory flavors go incredibly well with the juicy, succulent pork. Protein, fiber, vitamins, and minerals are all included in this meal in addition to its delicious flavor. Using a grill and butternut squash that has been expertly roasted, we'll demonstrate how to prepare and cook a pork tenderloin in this dish.

Ingredients:
- A pound of pork tenderloin
- Peeled, seeded, and cut into cubes, 1 small butternut squash
- 2 tablespoons of olive oil
- 1 teaspoon of salt

- Black pepper, 1/2 tsp.
- 1/2 teaspoon dried thyme
- 1/8 teaspoon of garlic powder

Instructions:

1. Medium-high heat should be set on the grill.
2. Salt, black pepper, thyme, garlic powder, and olive oil should all be combined in a bowl.

3. The mixture should be applied evenly to the pork tenderloin.

4. Cook the pork tenderloin for 12 to 15 minutes on each side or until it reaches an internal temperature of 145°F by placing it on the grill.

5. Set the oven to 400°F and start the grilling of the meat.

6. Sprinkle salt, pepper, and olive oil over the cubed butternut squash in a baking dish.

7. Once it is soft and lightly browned, roast the butternut squash for 20 to 25 minutes.

8. Once the pork has been taken off the grill, it should rest for five to ten minutes.

9. Roasted butternut squash is best served alongside the pork tenderloin.

Stew Made With Beans And Vegetables

A hearty, wholesome dish that is ideal for a chilly day is a stew made with chickpeas and vegetables. As a result of the stew's high protein and fiber content and absence of gluten, it is both vegan and gluten-free. With a side of rice or bread, it can be served alone or both ways.

Ingredients:
- Two teaspoons of olive oil
- Diced one large onion
- Three minced garlic cloves
- 1 tsp. cumin, ground
- 2 teaspoons of smoked paprika
- 1/2 tsp. coriander powder
- 0.5 teaspoons of cinnamon powder
- 1/8 tsp. of ground turmeric
- One-fourth of a teaspoon of cayenne
- Peeled and diced one large sweet potato
- 1 red bell pepper
- 1 yellow bell pepper
- 2 large carrots that have been peeled and diced
- 2 celery stalks,
- 1 can (15 oz) tomatoes, diced, in juice

- Chickpeas drained and rinsed, from one can (15 oz).
- 2 cups vegetable stock
- Salt and pepper
- Freshly chopped cilantro or parsley.

Instructions:

1. In a big pot on medium heat, warm the olive oil. Once the onion is soft and translucent, add the garlic and continue cooking for an additional 5 minutes while stirring occasionally.

2. The pot should now contain the spices (cumin, smoked paprika, coriander, cinnamon, turmeric, and cayenne pepper). Stir them in thoroughly. Spices should be fragrant after cooking for 1 to 2 minutes.

3. Red and yellow bell peppers, celery, carrots, and sweet potatoes should all be added to the pot and thoroughly mixed. Stirring once or twice, cook for 5 minutes.

4. Stir well after adding the vegetable broth, chickpeas, and diced tomatoes to the pot. To cook the vegetables until they are tender, bring the mixture to a boil, then lower the heat and simmer for 20 to 25 minutes.

5. Add salt and pepper to the stew's taste as desired.

6. With freshly chopped cilantro or parsley as a garnish, serve the stew hot.

7. Up to 5 days of refrigerator storage or three months of freezer storage are possible for this dish.

Brown Rice And Beef In a Stir-Fry

For a weeknight dinner, try this flavorful and nutritious stir-fry of beef and broccoli with brown rice. This dish is loaded with fiber, vitamins, and minerals as well as protein. An instruction manual for making this dish is provided below:

Ingredients:
- Thinly sliced against the grain 1 lb flank steak
- Three cups of broccoli florets
- Thinly sliced 1 red bell pepper
- Thinly sliced 1 yellow onion
- Garlic, minced from two cloves
- Two tablespoons of vegetable oil
- 1 tablespoon of cornstarch
- Low sodium soy sauce, one-fourth cup
- 1/fourth cup brown sugar
- 1 tablespoon sesame oil
- 2 cups of cooked brown rice

- 1/2 cup of beef broth

Instructions:

1. Get the beef ready first. Slice against the grain of the flank steak. The meat is kept tender and chewable thanks to this. Steer clear of the beef.

2. Put the cornstarch, soy sauce, brown sugar, sesame oil, and beef broth in a small bowl and whisk to combine. Dispose of.

3. Heat the vegetable oil to a medium-high temperature in a sizable skillet or wok. Add the chopped garlic and onion slices to the hot oil. To make the onions translucent, stir-fry for a minimum of two to three minutes.

4. The beef should be browned on all sides after you add it to the skillet and stir-fry for an additional 3 to 4 minutes.

5. To the skillet, add the red bell pepper slices and broccoli florets. until the vegetables are crisp-tender, stir-fry for an additional 2 to 3 minutes.

6. Give the beef and vegetables a generous helping of the soy sauce mixture. Continue to stir-fry the beef

and vegetables for an additional 1 to 2 minutes, or until the sauce thickens and covers them.

7. Cooked brown rice should be used as a bed for the beef and broccoli stir fry.

8. For a quick and simple lunch or dinner, this dish is ideal for meal prepping and reheats well.

Lamb Shepherd's Pie With Vegetables

A delicious and nutritious vegetarian version of the traditional shepherd's pie is made with lentils and vegetables. The lentils in this hearty dish provide protein, and the vegetables and creamy mashed potatoes on top are full of fiber and nutrients. In the colder months, it's ideal for a warm and comforting dinner.

Ingredients:
- A cup of lentils
- Three cups of vegetable stock
- 3 cloves of minced garlic
- 1 chopped onion
- 2 chopped carrots
- 2 chopped celery stalks
- 100 g of frozen peas
- 2 teaspoons of dried thyme
- 1 tsp. dried rosemary

- Salt and pepper
- Four cups of mashed potatoes
- 1/4 cup of shredded cheddar cheese (optional)

Instructions:

1. Your oven should be preheated at 375°F (190°C).

2. When the onion is translucent, add a little oil to a large skillet or pot and sauté the onion and garlic until translucent.

3. After adding them, cook the carrots and celery in the skillet for a few minutes, or until they begin to soften.

4. Bring the skillet to a boil after adding the lentils and vegetable broth. When the lentils are cooked, turn the heat down and let the mixture simmer for 20 to 25 minutes.

5. In the skillet, combine the salt, pepper, dried thyme, dried rosemary, and frozen peas.

6. To an expansive baking dish, add the lentil and vegetable mixture.

7. On top of the lentil and vegetable mixture, distribute the mashed potatoes evenly.

8. You can top the mashed potatoes with cheddar cheese shavings if you like.

9. When the filling is hot and bubbling and the mashed potatoes are just beginning to turn golden, bake for 25 to 30 minutes in the preheated oven.

Vegetable And Black Bean Filling For Baked Sweet Potatoes

A tasty and healthy meal can be made from baked sweet potatoes filled with a filling of hearty black beans and vegetables. This nutrient-rich, vegetarian dish is also free of gluten. Making it is as follows:

Ingredients:
- Four medium sweet potatoes
- Draining and rinsing one can of black beans
- 1 diced small onion
- 2 minced garlic cloves
- 1 diced zucchini
- 1 teaspoon cumin
- 1 teaspoon of chili powder
- 1 teaspoon of olive oil
- Salt, and pepper to taste

- Garnishes of fresh cilantro

Instructions:

1. Set the oven's temperature to 400 °F.
2. After cleaning, poke a fork through the sweet potatoes all over. Bake them for 45 to 50 minutes, or until they are tender, on a baking sheet.
3. Prepare the filling and bake the sweet potatoes concurrently. A big skillet with medium heat is used to warm the olive oil. About 2 minutes after adding them, the onion and garlic should be fragrant.
4. When the zucchini and red bell pepper are tender, add them to the skillet and cook for an additional 5 minutes.
5. Stir the black beans into the skillet after adding the cumin, chili powder, salt, and pepper. 5 more minutes of cooking should be done with sporadic stirring.
6. Remove the sweet potatoes from the oven once they are finished cooking and allow them to cool. Each potato should have a lengthwise slit cut through it. To widen the slit, gently push the ends of the potato together.
7. Add fresh cilantro on top after placing the filling inside each sweet potato.

Roasted Chicken With Tomatoes And Asparagus

For a family supper or weekend get-together, roast chicken with asparagus and tomatoes are a tasty and nutritious dish. Protein and vitamins abound in this dish, which is very simple to prepare. Asparagus and tomatoes bring a bright and fresh taste to the meal, and the roasted chicken is seasoned with a combination of herbs and spices that go well with the moist and soft flesh. Here are the steps to making roasted chicken with tomatoes and asparagus:

Ingredients:

- Chicken breasts, four
- Trimming and washing 1 pound of asparagus
- Cherry tomatoes in a pint, cleaned
- 1 tablespoon olive oil
- 1-tablespoon dried thyme
- 2 tablespoons dried rosemary
- 1 tablespoon of garlic powder
- 1 tablespoon paprika
- Salt and pepper.

Instructions:

1. Set the oven's temperature to 400 °F (200 °C).
2. Combine the paprika, dried garlic, dried rosemary, salt, and pepper in a small bowl.

3. The herb and spice mixture should be uniformly distributed over the chicken breasts, which should then be placed on a baking sheet. The chicken should then be well covered with the mixture.
4. Olive oil, salt, and pepper, to taste, should be drizzled over the cherry tomatoes and asparagus.
5. On the baking sheet, surround the chicken with the cherry tomatoes and seasoned asparagus.
6. Bake for 20 to 25 minutes in a preheated oven, or until the veggies are soft and faintly browned and the chicken is cooked through.

A Baked Cod Dish With Roasted Mixed Veggies

A tasty and nutritious dish that is simple to make is baked fish with roasted mixed veggies. As the mixed veggies are roasted with garlic and olive oil, the cod is seasoned with lemon, herbs, and spices. This recipe is excellent as a quick weeknight supper or as a healthy meal prep choice.

Ingredients:
- 4 cod fillets
- 1 lemon
- One tablespoon of olive oil
- 1 tsp. finely chopped fresh parsley
- 1 teaspoon finely chopped fresh thyme
- 1/4 teaspoon salt

- 1/8 tsp. black pepper
- 2 cups of mixed veggies (such as bell peppers, zucchini, and cherry tomatoes)
- Garlic, minced from two cloves

Instructions:

1. Set the oven's temperature to 400 °F.

2. Salt, pepper, and lemon juice are used to season the cod fillets. Dispose of.

3. Olive oil, garlic, salt, and pepper should all be combined with the mixed veggies in a big dish. When you are coating the veggies, keep stirring.

4. The vegetables should be tender and slightly browned after 20 to 25 minutes of baking, during which time they should be spread out on a baking sheet and stirred occasionally.

5. Open a large skillet and place it over medium-high heat while the vegetables are cooking. Add the cod fillets and cook for 3 to 4 minutes on each side, or until just lightly browned.

6.   Place the cooked cod fillets on the baking sheet alongside the roasted vegetables, nestling them in between the veggies.

7.   The remaining lemon juice should be squeezed over the vegetables and cod fillets. Parsley and thyme can also be added at this time.

8.   In order to fully cook the cod and turn the vegetables golden, place the baking sheet back in the oven and bake for an additional 8 to 10 minutes.

9.   With additional fresh herbs as a garnish, if desired, serve the baked cod and roasted vegetables hot.

Brown Rice And Vegetable And Tofu Curry

It is healthy and filling to eat this mouthwatering Tofu and Vegetable Curry. Anyone trying to eat less meat, including vegetarians, will find it to be ideal. It's a nutrient-dense meal because it's loaded with tofu's protein and a variety of vegetable fiber. Making it a flexible and flavorful meal, the recipe is also simple to adapt by adding your preferred vegetables and spices. Because it is more nutrient-dense and contains more fiber than white rice, brown rice is a healthier substitute for this recipe.

Ingredients:

- One cup of brown rice
- Drained and cut into cubes one package of firm tofu
- A single diced red onion
- Minced two garlic cloves
- 2 teaspoons curry powder
- One tomato-diced can
- 2 cups of various veggies (such as carrots, bell peppers, zucchini, and green beans)
- 1 cup vegetable stock
- Salt and pepper.
- Extra virgin olive oil

Instructions:

1. Set the oven to 375 degrees Fahrenheit.

2. Following the directions on the package, rinse the brown rice. Dispose of.

3. 1-2 tablespoons of extra virgin olive oil are heated over medium-high heat in a sizable skillet or wok.

4. In a skillet, combine the onion and garlic. Sauté for 2 to 3 minutes, or until the onion is translucent.

5. After adding the tofu, continue to cook the mixture of vegetables in the skillet for an additional 5 to 7

minutes, or until the vegetables are just beginning to soften.

6. Season with salt and pepper to taste before adding the curry powder.

7. The vegetable broth and tomato dice should be added to a can, then stirred together.

8. Heat should be set to medium-low after the mixture comes to a simmer. The vegetables should be soft and the flavors should have combined after 15-20 minutes of simmering the curry.

9. Add chopped cilantro or scallions as a garnish to the tofu and vegetable curry when serving it with brown rice.

Roasted Root Vegetables With Grilled Sirloin Steak

A satisfying and wholesome meal that's ideal for any occasion is grilled sirloin steak with roasted root vegetables. Iron, zinc, and vitamin B12 are all present in abundance in sirloin steak, lean meat that is also high in protein. This dish offers a range of vitamins, antioxidants, and fiber to support a healthy diet when combined with a variety of colorful root vegetables, like carrots, parsnips, and sweet potatoes. Making it is as follows:

Ingredients:
- One pound of sirloin steak
- 2 substantial carrots
- Parsnips, two
- Sweet potato
- One red onion
- 2 garlic cloves
- 2 tablespoons olive oil
- Salt and pepper.

Instructions:

1. Set your oven to 425 °F (218 °C).

2. The sweet potato, parsnips, and carrots should all be washed and peeled. Small, bite-sized pieces should be cut from them.

3. To make small pieces, peel and cut the onion.

4. Garlic should be peeled and finely chopped.

5. Vegetables that have been chopped, garlic, and olive oil should all be combined in a sizable bowl. Toss

the ingredients to coat evenly and season with salt and pepper to taste.

6. A baking sheet should have the vegetable mixture spread out in a single layer.

7. Vegetables should be roasted for 25 to 30 minutes in a preheated oven, or until they are soft and have a light browning. The vegetables should be stirred halfway through cooking to ensure even roasting.

8. Steak can be prepared while the vegetables are roasting. Add salt and pepper to the steak as desired.

9. To medium-high heat, preheat a grill pan or an outdoor grill.

10. The steak should be cooked for 3 to 4 minutes on each side, depending on how well done you like it.

11. After the steak has finished cooking, turn off the heat and let it rest for a while before slicing.

12. Put the roasted root vegetables on the side and serve the steak sliced.

Turkey Meatballs Over Zucchini Noodles With Tomato Sauce

As compared to typical pasta, zucchini noodles, or "zoodles," are a low-carb and nutritious option. For people with gluten allergies or who wish to reduce their carb intake, they're a fantastic alternative. With zucchini noodles, turkey meatballs, and homemade tomato sauce, we'll make a tasty and wholesome supper.

Ingredients:
- Two little spiralized zucchini
- A single can of crushed tomatoes
- One tablespoon of olive oil
- Two cloves of garlic, minced
- One small onion.
- One teaspoon of dried basil
- A tsp. of dried oregano
- 1/8 teaspoon dried red pepper flakes
- Salt and pepper.
- A pound of pounded turkey
- A quarter cup of almond flour
- 1 egg
- Parmesan cheese, grated, one-fourth cup
- Fresh parsley, cut into two teaspoons.
- Salt and pepper.

Instructions:

1. Your oven should be preheated at 375°F (190°C).

2. Ground turkey, almond flour, egg, Parmesan cheese, parsley, salt, and pepper should all be mixed together in a big mixing basin. All ingredients should be thoroughly mixed before serving.

3. Make meatballs between 1 and 2 inches in diameter out of the turkey mixture.

4. In order to properly cook through and brown the meatballs, place them on a baking sheet that has been prepared with parchment paper and bake for 15-20 minutes.

5. Warm up the oil in a big pan over medium heat while the meatballs are baking. For about 3 to 4 minutes, add the minced garlic and onion and sauté them until they are aromatic and tender.

6. To the skillet, add the red pepper flakes, dried oregano, dry basil, smashed tomatoes, salt, and pepper. Let the sauce boil for 10 to 15 minutes, or until it has thickened, after thoroughly combining all the ingredients.

7. Heat 1 tablespoon of olive oil over medium-high heat in a separate skillet. While you toss occasionally for two to three minutes, add the spiralized zucchini noodles and cook until they are soft.

Tomato Sauce And Turkey Meatballs Topped With Zucchini Noodles

With a mixed greens salad, baked portobello mushrooms are packed.

For a tasty and nutritious vegetarian dish that is suitable for lunch or supper, try baked-filled portobello mushrooms. A number of items may be stuffed with portobello mushrooms, which are big, meaty mushrooms. In this dish, they will be stuffed with a mixture of quinoa, spinach, and feta cheese and served with a mixed greens salad.

Ingredients:
- 4 substantial portobello mushrooms
- A cup of quinoa
- 2 cups spinach
- Feta cheese, broken up into 1/2 cup.
- Garlic, minced from two cloves
- One tablespoon of olive oil
- Salt and pepper
- Mixed-green salad

Instructions:

1. The oven should be heated to 375°F (190°C).

2. The portobello mushrooms should have their stems removed, and a spoon should be used to remove the gills. A baking sheet should be used for the mushrooms.

3. 2 cups of water should be heated up in a pot. To cook the quinoa and allow the water to be absorbed, add the quinoa, lower the heat to low, cover the pan, and simmer for 15 to 20 minutes.

4. Make the olive oil warm in a pan over medium heat while the quinoa is cooking. For 1-2 minutes, until aromatic, add the minced garlic and cook.

5. In the skillet, add the spinach and cook for two to three minutes, or until wilted.

6. Once the quinoa has finished cooking, add the feta cheese and quinoa to the pan. Add salt and pepper to taste after thoroughly combining everything.

7. Place the quinoa mixture within the crowns of each portobello mushroom, pushing it down firmly.

8. For 20 to 25 minutes in the oven, or until the filling is well cooked through, bake the stuffed mushrooms.

9. Making a mixed greens salad by combining your favorite salad greens with a mild vinaigrette can help you pass the time while the mushrooms are roasting.

10. The mixed greens salad should be served with hot-filled mushrooms.

Whole-Grain Tortillas With Chicken And Veggie Fajitas

Using whole-grain tortillas with chicken and veggie fajitas makes for a tasty and nutritious supper that can be enjoyed every night of the week. The chicken, carrots, and tortillas in this recipe are excellent sources of whole grains and are also filled with protein and other minerals. The fajitas may be easily customized to your preferences by using different veggies or seasonings.

Ingredients:
- 2 chicken breasts without the bones or the skin.
- 1 bell pepper, red
- 1 pepper, green
- 1 onion
- 2 tablespoons olive oil

- pepper powder, 1 tbsp
- Cucumber, 1 teaspoon
- 1 tablespoon of smoked paprika
- Garlic powder, 1/2 teaspoon
- When desired, add salt and pepper.
- 4 whole-wheat tortillas

Instructions:

1. Set your oven's temperature to 350 °F (175 °C).

2. Red, green, and onion into thin strips, together with the chicken breasts, have been washed.

3. Cumin, smoked paprika, garlic powder, salt, and pepper should all be combined in a small bowl with the chili powder.

4. A big skillet with medium-high heat is used to heat 1 tablespoon of olive oil. For about 5 minutes, or until the chicken is well cooked, add the chicken.

5. Place the chicken aside after removing it from the skillet.

6. Sliced peppers and onions are added along with another tablespoon of olive oil to the same skillet. until the veggies are soft, 3 to 4 minutes of sautéing.

7. In the pan with the veggies, re-add the cooked chicken.

8. The chicken and veggies should be well-coated after being sprinkled with the seasoned mixture.

9. After placing the chicken and vegetable combination in a baking dish, preheat the oven to 400°F. Bake the mixture for 10 to 12 minutes, or until the chicken is well cooked through and the veggies have developed a light caramelization.

10. Warm up the whole grain tortillas for 30 seconds in the microwave or a few minutes in the oven while the fajita mixture bakes.

11. Enjoy eating the warm tortillas and chicken and veggie fajita combination! If preferred, you may top the dish with ingredients like sour cream, chopped avocado, or shredded cheese.

Quinoa- And Roasted Vegetable-Topped Fish In The Oven

Quinoa-based baked salmon dish with roasted veggies and quinoa is a filling and healthful lunch or supper option. Protein, omega-3 fatty acids, fiber, and a range of vitamins and minerals are just a few of the nutrients that are abundant in this meal. Making it is as follows:

Ingredients:
- Two salmon filets (about 6 oz each)
- 1 cup drained and washed quinoa
- 2 cups of diced
- Bite-sized mixed veggies, such as broccoli, bell peppers, and carrots.
- 1 tablespoon olive oil
- Salt and pepper.
- Lemon wedges

Instructions:

1. Set the oven's temperature to 400 °F (200 °C).
2. Baking sheets should be lined with aluminum foil or parchment paper.
3. To make room for the veggies, leave enough space between the salmon fillets on one side of the baking sheet.
4. Use salt and pepper to season the fish.
5. Add olive oil, salt, and pepper to taste, and toss the mixed veggies in a bowl.
6. Vegetables should be arranged on the baking sheet's opposite side.

7. Cook the salmon in the oven for 15 to 20 minutes, or until it is well cooked, and the veggies are soft and gently browned.
8. Prepare the quinoa per package directions while the salmon and veggies are baking.
9. On a bed of quinoa, plate the salmon with the veggies.
10. Salmon and veggies should be served with lemon slices on top.

Brown Rice Noodles And Vegetables In a Stir-Fry

A simple and nutritious supper that is flavorful and nutrient-rich is this stir-fry of vegetables and tofu with brown rice noodles. It's an excellent way to obtain your recommended daily intake of veggies and plant-based protein, and because it uses brown rice noodles, it is also a gluten-free choice. Also, you may simply adapt this cuisine to your tastes and dietary requirements.

Ingredients:
- 1 box of brown rice noodles
- 1 cubed, drained, and cubed piece of firm tofu
- 1 sliced red bell pepper 1 sliced yellow onion
- 2-cups worth of broccoli florets
- One cup of sliced mushrooms
- Garlic, minced from 2 cloves
- 2 teaspoons of vegetable oil

- A quarter cup of tamari or soy sauce
- Two teaspoons of rice vinegar
- 1 teaspoon of honey
- 1 tablespoon cornstarch
- Salt and pepper.

Instructions:

1. Follow the directions on the box for cooking the brown rice noodles. Set aside after draining.
2. Soy sauce, tamari, rice vinegar, honey, and cornstarch should all be combined in a small basin. Dispose of.

3. Large skillet or wok over medium-high heat to warm the vegetable oil.

4. For 5-7 minutes, or until golden brown on both sides, add the cubed tofu. Put aside after being removed from the skillet.

5. In the same skillet, add the sliced mushrooms, red bell pepper, onion, and broccoli florets. When the veggies are crunchy but still soft, cook for 5-7 minutes.

6. After stirring for 30 seconds, add the minced garlic to the skillet and heat until fragrant.

7. Replacing the cooked tofu with the soy sauce mixture, and add the skillet with everything to it. Vegetables and tofu should be well coated in sauce after stirring.

8. Once the sauce has thickened, cook for a further 2 to 3 minutes.

9. Put the cooked brown rice noodles on top of the stir fry.

A Mixed Green Salad With Beef And Veggie Chili

An excellent and filling dish for chilly days is beef and vegetable chili. As a nutritious and filling supper alternative, this meal is loaded with veggies and lean protein. For a complete and wholesome dinner, serve it with a side of mixed greens salad.

Ingredients:
- One pound of ground beef
- Diced 1 onion
- Minced two garlic cloves
- A pair of chopped bell peppers
- A single chopped and seeded jalapeño pepper
- Drained and rinsed one can of kidney beans.
- One tomato-diced can

- 1/4 cup chili powder
- Cumin, 1 teaspoon
- A half-teaspoon of paprika
- Salt and pepper.
- 25% of a cup of chopped fresh cilantro
- One tablespoon of olive oil
- Dish of a greens mixture

Instructions:

1. Over medium-high heat, preheat a large saucepan. To the saucepan, add olive oil.

2. To the saucepan, add the minced garlic and chopped onions. Cook for 5 minutes, or until the vegetables are tender.

3. Adding the ground beef, simmer for 8 to 10 minutes, or until browned.

4. Cook for a further 5 minutes after adding the diced bell peppers and jalapeño pepper, in minced form.

5. The kidney beans should be drained, then add the can of chopped tomatoes.

6. To the saucepan, add salt, pepper, paprika, cumin, and chili powder. To thoroughly incorporate all ingredients, stir well.

7. The mixture should be brought to a boil, then the heat should be turned down so that the mixture simmers for 20 to 30 minutes, or until the veggies are soft and the flavors have combined.

8. Add fresh cilantro that has been chopped.

9. With a side of mixed greens salad, serve hot.

Green Beans And Baked Pork Chops With Roasted Sweet Potatoes

It's simple to prepare a wonderful and nutritious meal of baked pork chops with roasted sweet potatoes and green beans. For a well-rounded supper, the oven-baked pork chops are served with roasted sweet potatoes and green beans. An instructional recipe for this meal is provided below:

Ingredients:
- 4 bone-in chops of pork
- Cubed and peeled two medium sweet potatoes
- Trimmed 1 pound of green beans

- Two teaspoons of olive oil
- 2 teaspoons of dried thyme
- 1 tsp. of garlic powder
- Salt and pepper.

Instructions:

1. On a baking sheet, spread parchment paper and preheat the oven to 400°F (200°C).
2. Mix the olive oil, garlic powder, salt, and pepper in a bowl along with the dried thyme.
3. Toss the green beans and sweet potatoes in the olive oil mixture and spread them out on the baking sheet.
4. After evenly distributing them, arrange the veggies in a baking dish. Bake for 20 to 25 minutes, or until the vegetables are soft, tossing them midway through.
5. Pork chops should be seasoned with salt and pepper to taste while the veggies are roasting.
6. The pork chops are put in a big pan that has been heated to medium-high heat. Cook until browned, about 2 to 3 minutes per side.
7. After the pork chops are on the baking sheet with the roasted veggies, bake them for a further 10-15 minutes, or until they achieve an internal temperature of 145°F (63°C).
8. Pork chops should sit for five minutes after being taken out of the oven before being served.

9. Roasted sweet potatoes and green beans should be served alongside the pork chops.

30 Recipes For Snacks

Apples Cut Into Wedges With Almond Butter

A nutritious and scrumptious snack that is ideal for any time of the day is apple slices with almond butter. A wonderful supply of protein and healthy fats is almond butter, while apples are a fantastic source of fiber and antioxidants. Any age group may appreciate this straightforward snack, which is also simple to make.

Ingredients:
- One medium apple
- 2 teaspoons of almond butter
- Honey, cinnamon, and chopped nuts are optional additions.

Instructions:

1. To get thin, uniform slices, slice the apple after washing. Core and seeds should be removed.
2. On top of each apple slice, apply a coating of almond butter.
3. On top of the almond butter, you can optionally sprinkle some cinnamon, honey, or chopped nuts.

4. Put the apple slices in a serving dish and start serving right away.

Bell Pepper Slices And a Hard-Boiled Egg

For a quick breakfast on the go or a simple noon energy boost, hard-boiled eggs are a simple and nourishing snack. A filling and well-balanced snack full of protein, fiber, and vitamins may be made by combining them with thinly sliced bell pepper. In addition to being simple to make, this snack is low in calories.

Instructions:

5. Boil the eggs first, then. The eggs should be placed in a saucepan with just an inch or so of water covering them.

6. Over a high flame, bring the water to a boil. Put a lid on the pot after the water has boiled, then turn off the heat.

7. Depending on how well done you want your eggs, let the eggs sit in the boiling water for 9 to 12 minutes.

8. Bell pepper should be cut into thin strips and prepared while the eggs are cooking.

9. To stop the cooking of the eggs when they have finished frying, remove the hot water from the pan and replace it with cool water.

10. Gently tap the cooled eggs on a hard surface to shatter the shell, then peel the shell off.

11. Place the rounds of hard-boiled eggs on a platter after slicing them.

12. Next to the eggs on the platter, arrange the sliced bell pepper.

13. The eggs and bell pepper should be taste-tested with a touch of salt and pepper.

Berries And Chopped Almonds With Greek Yogurt

A tasty and nutritious breakfast or snack choice is Greek yogurt with berries and chopped almonds. Berries offer antioxidants and fiber, Greek yogurt is strong in protein, low in fat, and packed with probiotics, while nuts are an excellent source of healthy fats and extra protein. Berries also give antioxidants. You may add your favorite berries and nuts to this straightforward and simple-to-make dish to suit your preferences and enjoy it at any time of the day.

Ingredients:
- One cup of Greek yogurt
- 0.5 cup of mixed berries (strawberries, blueberries, raspberries, blackberries)
- 1/4 cup chopped nuts (almonds, pecans, walnuts)

Instructions:

- The berries should be thoroughly cleaned with running water and dried with paper towels. Little strawberry chunks should be cut.
- Greek yogurt should be put in a small bowl and blended well.
- Over the yogurt, scatter the mixed berries.
- The berries are covered with chopped nuts.
- Don't wait to serve; savor it!

Note: For meal preparation purposes, you may alternatively keep the yogurt, berries, and almonds in the refrigerator separately and combine them when you're ready to eat.

Hummus And Carrot Sticks

A quick and wholesome snack that goes well with any time of the day is carrot sticks and hummus. A delightful and nourishing snack that anybody may enjoy is made possible by the marriage of crisp carrots and creamy hummus. The low-calorie, high-fiber, and high-protein nature of this snack makes it a fantastic choice for anybody trying to lose weight. The preparation of carrot sticks with hummus is described in detail here.

Ingredients:
- Few medium-sized carrots
- Hummus, half a cup
- Salt and pepper.

Instructions:

1. Clean and peel the carrots. Tops and bottoms should be removed and thrown away.

2. Long, thin sticks made out of carrots. In order to acquire the correct form, you can use a knife or a vegetable peeler.

3. A dish or container can be used to hold the carrot sticks.

4. To a small bowl, add 1/2 cup of hummus.

5. Add salt and pepper to taste for hummus-making.

6. the seasoned hummus and carrot stick together.

7. Enjoy the hummus with the carrot sticks!

Tips:

*   Hummus comes in two varieties: homemade and pre-made.
*   Try hummus made with roasted red pepper or garlic or other flavored varieties.
*   Before serving, add some chopped fresh herbs, such as parsley or cilantro, to the hummus if you want to give it a little additional flavor.

Cut-Up Cucumbers With Tzatziki

For a light mid-day or evening snack, try cucumber slices with tzatziki. It's a delicious and healthful combination. Garlic, dill, and lemon juice flavor the Greek yogurt foundation of the tzatziki sauce. For dipping veggies, crackers, or pita chips, this low-calorie and low-fat dip are excellent.

Ingredients:
*   1 big cucumber
*   1 cup of unflavored Greek yogurt
*   Cucumbers, grated, half a cup
*   1 tablespoon of fresh dill and 2 minced garlic cloves
*   Salt and pepper.

Instructions:

1. Making the tzatziki sauce should be done first. Combine the Greek yogurt, cucumber, garlic, dill, and lemon juice in a medium mixing basin. To mix, thoroughly combine.

2. Salt and pepper to taste, and add to the tzatziki sauce. In order for the flavors to come together, chill the tzatziki sauce for at least 30 minutes.

3. Cucumber preparation involves cleaning it and slicing it into tiny pieces while the tzatziki sauce chills.

4. Tzatziki sauce should be taken out of the refrigerator after it has chilled and given a brief whisk.

5. On a platter, arrange the cucumber slices, and provide the tzatziki sauce on the side for dipping. Enjoy!

Tips:

- Dried dill can be used in its place if fresh dill is unavailable.
- To change the tzatziki sauce's flavor to your preference, you may also use additional herbs or spices, including cumin or mint.

Sea-Salted Edamame

Made from immature soybeans that are collected before they have fully hardened, edamame is a well-liked snack in Japan. Protein, fiber, vitamins, and minerals may all be found in abundance in edamame. It may be used as a protein-packed addition to salads and stir-fries or as a healthful snack.

Ingredients:
- Frozen edamame in a cup
- Half-teaspoon of sea salt

Instructions:

1. Water is being heated in a pot.
2. In a pot of boiling water, add the frozen edamame, and simmer for three to five minutes, or until soft.
3. The edamame should be rinsed in a colander with cold water to help them cool down.
4. Sea salt should be added to the edamame, then coated.
5. As an appetizer or snack, serve the edamame right away.

Notes:
To give them a crispy texture, edamame can also be baked. Edamame should be roasted in a 400°F oven for

10 to 15 minutes, or until crispy, after being tossed with a little olive oil and sea salt.

To give edamame more taste, you may also season them with other ingredients like soy sauce, sesame oil, or garlic powder.

Nuts With Dried Apricots

When you want a fast energy boost or a pleasant lunchtime snack, almonds, and dried apricots make a delicious and nutritious snack that will satisfy your cravings. Dried apricots are rich in vitamins and minerals, such as potassium and vitamin A, while almonds are a fantastic source of fiber, protein, and healthy fats. Here's how to prepare this straightforward snack:

Ingredients:
1/4 cup of raw almonds
1/4 cup of dried apricots

Instructions:

1) Almonds that are fresh and dried apricots totaling 1/4 cup each.
2) For the purpose of getting rid of any dirt or debris, rinse the almonds in cold water.

3) Fill a small dish or container with the almonds and dried apricots.
4) In order to spread them equally, combine the almonds and apricots.
5) Sip a cup of tea or coffee while you enjoy them as a snack on your own.

Notes:
- Before combining the almonds and apricots, roast the almonds in the oven at 350°F (175°C) for 8 to 10 minutes if you want them to be lightly toasted.
- To stay away from additional sugars, be sure to select dried apricots that are unsweetened.

Cheese Ricotta And Sliced Pears

Simple and tasty, sliced pear with ricotta cheese makes a quick snack. In contrast to ricotta cheese, which is a wonderful source of calcium and protein, pears are a fantastic provider of fiber and vitamins. For a small dessert or afternoon pick-me-up, this snack is ideal.

Ingredients:
- 1 pear that is ripe
- 1/4 cup of ricotta cheese
- Honey (optional)

Instructions:

1. Pears should be cleaned and thinly sliced.
2. In a small bowl, combine the ricotta cheese and mash it with a fork to combine the ingredients.
3. Over the pear slices, if preferred, pour honey.
4. Ricotta cheese should be topped with pear pieces when serving.
5. Have pleasure in your delicious and healthy snack!

Options:
- To enhance flavor, sprinkle the dish with cinnamon or nutmeg.
- Don't use pears; instead, substitute apples or peaches.
- Cottage cheese or Greek yogurt can be used in place of ricotta cheese.

Bell Peppers, Sliced, And Guacamole

A nutritious and scrumptious snack that can be eaten at any time is sliced bell pepper with guacamole. This is a nutrient-dense and satiating choice for a snack since it is packed in fiber, good fats, and vitamins. The following recipe pairs guacamole with sliced bell pepper:

Ingredients:
- Sliced 1 avocado
- 1 bell pepper
- Juiced half a lime

- A finely minced quarter of an onion
- One tiny tomato
- 1/8 tsp. black pepper
- Finely chopped fresh cilantro.

Instructions:

1. Bell pepper slices should be thinly cut and placed on a platter for later.

2. Avocado and lime juice should be put in a mixing dish. Use a fork to thoroughly mash the avocado.

3. Mix thoroughly after adding the tomato and onion, which have been finely diced.

4. Add pepper and salt to taste when guacamole is prepared. To thoroughly blend, stir.

5. Place the bell pepper slices and guacamole on a dish. If desired, garnish with chopped cilantro.

This treatment is ideal as an afternoon snack or for celebrations. By varying the amount of lime juice, salt, or pepper, you can adapt it to your preference and it is simple to prepare. To the creamy guacamole, the thinly sliced bell pepper brings a pleasant crunch and sweetness.

Mozzarella Cheese And Tomato Slices

A quick and easy snack or appetizer is sliced tomato with fresh mozzarella. It is a simple but delicious combination. It is a traditional Italian pairing, ideal for a summer day, to combine ripe, juicy tomatoes with creamy, tangy mozzarella cheese. Vitamin C, calcium, and protein are just a few of the nutrients that make up this snack. To make sliced tomato and fresh mozzarella, follow the instructions provided here.

Ingredients:
- Two ripe tomatoes.
- 4 oz. fresh mozzarella cheese
- 1 tablespoon olive oil
- Salt and pepper.
- Leafy fresh basil (optional)

Instructions:

1. The tomatoes should be cleaned and dried. Round the tomato slices to a thickness of 1/4 inch.
2. Additionally, cut rounds of fresh mozzarella cheese to a thickness of 1/4 inch.
3. Slices of fresh mozzarella cheese should slightly overlap the tomato slices as you alternate them on a plate.

4. The tomato and cheese slices should be covered in olive oil.
5. Don't forget to season with salt and pepper.
6. Adding fresh basil leaves as a garnish is optional.
7. Don't wait to serve; savor it!

In addition to being quick and simple to prepare, this snack can be tailored to your preferences. You can change up the cheese by using a different kind, or you can add more flavor by drizzling honey or balsamic vinegar on top. At a get-together or potluck, it makes a wonderful snack to share with friends and family.

With Sliced Peaches And Cottage Cheese

A quick and wholesome snack that is great any time of day is cottage cheese and sliced peaches. The peaches' sweetness balances the cottage cheese's tangy flavor, and this snack is a good source of calcium and protein. Using sliced peaches, make cottage cheese as follows:

Ingredients:
- Cottage cheese, 1/2 cup
- 1 sliced medium-sized peach

Instructions:

1. The peach should be washed and thinly cut.

2. In a bowl or on a plate, spoon the cottage cheese.
3. Top the cottage cheese with the peach slices.
4. Right away serve.

Peanut Butter On Celery Sticks

A traditional snack that's tasty and nutrient-rich is celery sticks with peanut butter. Compared to peanut butter, celery has more fiber and fewer calories, while peanut butter offers protein and good fats. You can eat them together to create a filling snack that will give you energy all day.

Ingredients:
- A stalk of celery
- Original peanut butter (creamy or crunchy)

Instructions:
1. Before cutting off the ends, wash the celery sticks. Smaller, 3–4 inch pieces of the stalks should be cut off.
2. One side of the celery stick should be covered with a spoonful of peanut butter. Depending on your preference, use peanut butter that is either creamy or crunchy.
3. The remaining peanut butter and celery sticks should be prepared in the same manner.
4. Your tasty and healthy snack is ready to be served.

5. You can also add toppings like raisins, sliced almonds, or honey for more sweetness and crunch.

Rubbed Chickpeas

You can eat roasted chickpeas at any time of the day as a tasty and nutritious snack. They make a fantastic substitute for chips or other processed snacks because they are a great source of protein and fiber. Using up a can of chickpeas that you might have in your pantry by roasting them is another excellent idea. You can make crispy roasted chickpeas using just a few basic ingredients, as we will demonstrate in this recipe.

Ingredients:
*   1 can chickpeas
*   1 teaspoon of olive oil
*   Half a teaspoon of paprika
*   One-quarter teaspoon of garlic powder
*   1/8 teaspoon salt

Instructions:

1. Your oven should be preheated at 400°F (200°C).

2. After draining the liquid, open the chickpea can. Using a paper towel, dry the chickpeas after giving them a cold water rinse.

3. Combine the salt, garlic powder, paprika, and olive oil in a small bowl.

4. To evenly coat the chickpeas, add them to the bowl with the spice mixture and toss.

5. A baking sheet should have the chickpeas spread out in a single layer.

6. Until they are crispy and golden brown, bake the chickpeas for 20 to 30 minutes. To ensure that the chickpeas cook uniformly, stir them after every 10 minutes.

7. Following their removal from the oven, the chickpeas should be given some time to cool.

8. As a side dish or a garnish for salads, soups, and other dishes, you can use roasted chickpeas.

Slices Of Apple And Cheese

A straightforward and delicious snack that is suitable for any time of the day is cheese and apple slices. It is a satisfying and nutritious treat because of the sourness of the cheese and the sweetness of the apple blend so well.

To make cheese and apple slices, follow these instructions:

Ingredients:
- One medium apple
- Two to three slices of your preferred cheese

Instructions:

1. Remove any seeds or stems before washing the apple and slicing it into thin rounds.
2. Similarly sized to the apple slices, cut the cheese into slices.
3. For each apple slice, place a slice of cheese on top.
4. If desired, you can broil the cheese and apple slices in the oven for a couple of minutes, just long enough for the cheese to melt and bubble.
5. Enjoy after serving!

Variations:
- Use a variety of cheeses, such as goat cheese, brie, or cheddar.
- To give the apple slices more flavor, top them with cinnamon.
- To give the cheese a bit of sweetness, top it with a dollop of honey or jam.
- Add some crunch by topping it with chopped nuts or seeds.

Cucumber And Turkey Wraps

Served at a party or as a quick snack, turkey, and cucumber roll-ups are a straightforward but flavorful food option. Its high protein content and low-calorie content make it a filling and healthy choice.

Ingredients:
- Four large slices of turkey
- A single cucumber thinly sliced lengthwise
- 4 tbsp. of cream cheese
- Salt and pepper.

Instructions:

1. On a cutting board, arrange the slices of turkey.
2. Each slice should have one tablespoon of cream cheese distributed evenly over it.
3. Each slice should have a thin border around the edges before adding a few cucumber strips.
4. According to taste, add salt and pepper.
5. Make sure the filling is well-enclosed in each slice of turkey as you tightly roll it up.
6. Make bite-sized cuts in the roll-ups with a sharp knife.
7. Enjoy after serving!

Note: You can change up this recipe by using various deli types of meat or by adding additional fillings like sliced cheese or avocado.

Blended Nuts And Seeds

At any time of the day, mixed nuts and seeds make a tasty and healthy snack. They are a wonderful source of protein, fiber, healthy fats, and vitamins and minerals that are needed for good health. They are a convenient snack choice for people who are busy, and they are also simple to transport.

Directions in detail:

1) Select the nuts and seeds of your choice. Almonds, walnuts, cashews, peanuts, pumpkin seeds, sunflower seeds, and chia seeds are some of the more well-liked alternatives.

2) Set your oven's temperature to 350 °F (175 °C).

3) On a baking sheet, distribute the nuts and seeds evenly.

4) Until lightly toasted and fragrant, bake the nuts and seeds for 8 to 10 minutes. Make sure they are being watched to prevent burning.

5) The nuts and seeds should cool completely after being removed from the oven.

6) For storage, place the nuts and seeds in a sealable plastic bag or another airtight container.

7) To add flavor and nutrition to salads, yogurt, oatmeal, or smoothie bowls, you can add your mixed nuts and seeds as a snack or as an addition to other dishes.

Sliced Roasted Sweet Potatoes

Sweet potato wedges roasted in the oven make a tasty, wholesome, and quick snack or side dish. The high fiber, vitamin, and mineral content of sweet potatoes makes them a wholesome addition to any meal.

Ingredients:
- 1 large and 2 medium sweet potatoes
- Two teaspoons of olive oil
- Paprika and salt, each in a teaspoon
- 0.5 teaspoons of garlic powder

Instructions:

1. On a baking sheet, spread parchment paper and preheat the oven to 400°F (200°C).

2. The sweet potatoes should be thoroughly cleaned before being cut into wedges of a similar size and thickness.

3. Combine the salt, garlic powder, paprika, and olive oil in a small bowl.

4. Spread the olive oil mixture over the sweet potato wedges in a sizable mixing bowl. To coat the wedges evenly, use a spoon or your hands.

5. The prepared baking sheet should have the sweet potato wedges laid out in a single layer.

6. Bake the sweet potato wedges for 25 to 30 minutes, or until they are soft and have a light brown exterior.

7. When ready to serve, take it out of the oven and let it cool briefly. Enjoy!

8. The flavor of your sweet potato wedges can be altered by adding additional seasonings like chili powder, cumin, or rosemary. You can also serve them with a dipping sauce, such as ranch or aioli, to give them more flavor.

Grilling Zucchini And Adding Feta Cheese

A delicious and healthy side dish that goes well with any meal is grilled zucchini and feta cheese. A tangy and salty flavor is added to the dish by the feta cheese, which also adds nutrients to the dish's nutrient-dense, low-calorie, and high-fiber zucchini. Any main course can be served with this straightforward, simple-to-make recipe as a side dish.

Ingredients:
- Sliced lengthwise into 1/4-inch-thick pieces
- 2 medium zucchini
- Two teaspoons of olive oil
- 1/8 teaspoon of salt
- 1/8 tsp. black pepper
- Feta cheese, chopped into 1/4 cup
- 1 tsp. finely chopped fresh parsley

Instructions:

1. Medium-high heat should be set on the grill.

2. Combine the black pepper, salt, and olive oil in a small bowl.

3. Apply the olive oil mixture to both sides of the slices of zucchini.

4. Slices of zucchini should be grilled for two to three minutes per side, or until they are tender and lightly charred.

5. The zucchini slices should be taken off the grill and placed on a serving platter.

6. Slices of zucchini are covered with feta cheese crumbles.

7. Sliced fresh parsley is a good garnish.

8. Don't wait to serve; savor it!

The recipe can also be prepared in a grill pan or on a stovetop griddle if you don't have a grill. Simply place the griddle or pan over medium-high heat and cook the zucchini slices as you would on the grill.

Cherry Tomatoes Glazed With Balsamic Vinegar And Fresh Basil

A delicious and healthful snack or side dish is made with cherry tomatoes, fresh basil, and balsamic sauce. It's impossible to resist the delicious flavor combination of tart balsamic glaze, aromatic basil, and sweet cherry tomatoes. Easy to prepare and great as a side dish for any dinner, this recipe is great for a fast snack.

Ingredients:
- One pint of cherry tomatoes
- One tablespoon of olive oil
- Both salt and pepper
- Two teaspoons of balsamic glaze
- One-fourth cup of chopped fresh basil leaves

Instructions:

1. Set the oven's temperature to 400 °F (200 °C).

2. The cherry tomatoes should be washed and dried off.

3. A baking dish should be filled with cherry tomatoes and oil. Toss to coat after adding salt and pepper.

4. For 15 to 20 minutes, or until the tomatoes begin to burst and take on a light caramelization, roast the tomatoes in the preheated oven.

5. In the meantime, take the tomatoes out of the oven and let them cool.

6. After drizzling the roasted cherry tomatoes with balsamic glaze, top with chopped fresh basil leaves.

7. As a snack or side dish, serve the cherry tomatoes warm.

Popcorn With Nutritional Yeast

Every time of the day is a great opportunity to consume popcorn, a beloved and nutritious snack. It has a high fiber content and is simple to flavor to your liking. By sprinkling nutritional yeast, a vegan source of vitamin B12 with a nutty, cheesy flavor, over top of popcorn, one may enjoy it in a healthy and delicious way. To make popcorn using nutritional yeast, follow these instructions:

Ingredients:
- Popcorn kernels in a half-cup
- One tablespoon of olive oil
- 2-tablespoons-worth of nutritious yeast
- Taste-tested salt

Instructions:

1. 350°F (180°C) should be the oven's preheated temperature.
2. Fill a big bowl with popcorn kernels.
3. Popcorn kernels should be covered in oil after being drizzled with olive oil and stirred.
4. On a baking sheet, distribute the popcorn grains evenly.
5. Until the kernels begin to pop, bake the popcorn in the oven for about 10 minutes.
6. As soon as the popcorn has finished popping, take it out of the oven and top it with the nutritional yeast.
7. To equally distribute salt and nutritional yeast on the popcorn, add salt to taste and toss the mixture.

8. You may either serve the popcorn right away or save it for later in an airtight container.
9. Snack on some popcorn with nutritional yeast for a wonderful and nutritious meal or snack.

Baking Kale Chips

Easy to prepare at home, baked kale chips are a nutritious and delectable snack. Baking kale into crunchy chips is a terrific way to enjoy its health benefits. Kale is a super-food rich in vitamins, minerals, and fiber. This snack can quell the desire for something crunchy and salty and is also low in calories.

Ingredients:
• One bunch of kale.
• One tablespoon of olive oil
• Salt and pepper.
• Garlic powder and nutritional yeast are optional spices.

Instructions:

1. Set your oven's temperature to 350 °F (175 °C).
2. Using a fresh kitchen towel or paper towel, thoroughly dry the kale leaves after washing.
3. To make the kale leaves into bite-sized pieces, cut off the stems.

4. The olive oil should be added to the chopped kale in a mixing dish. Kale leaves should be evenly covered with oil by massaging your hands into them.
5. Add any other ingredients you like to the kale, along with salt and pepper.
6. On a parchment, paper-lined baking sheet spread the kale pieces out in a single layer.
7. Roast the kale in the oven for 10-15 minutes, or until it is crispy and lightly browned. When the cooking process comes to a close, watch them carefully to prevent burning.
8. As soon as the kale chips are done baking, remove them from the oven and allow them cool.
9. If not serving right away, you can keep it for up to a few days in an airtight container.

Berry And Nut-Chopped Cottage Cheese

With almonds and berries, cottage cheese makes a delicious protein-rich snack. It's simple to create this snack, which also happens to be delicious and healthful.

Ingredients:
- Cottage cheese, half a cup
- A quarter cup of chopped mixed nuts (such as almonds, walnuts, and pecans)
- 1/8 cup mixed berries (such as strawberries, blueberries, and raspberries)

Instructions:

1. Cottage cheese should be poured into a small bowl after being weighed out to be 1/2 cup.
2. The mixed nuts should be cleaned and chopped before being added to the cottage cheese. Blend well.
3. The mixed berries should be washed, cut up, and added to the cottage cheese mixture. Blend well.
4. As a wholesome and mouthwatering snack, dish up the cottage cheese combination in a bowl.
5. In addition, you may use your preferred nuts and berries and pour some honey on top for sweetness.

Berry, Almond Milk, And Chia Seed-Based Low-Gi Smoothie

A tasty and nutritious snack or meal replacement is a smoothie with a low glycemic index (GI) that is created with berries, almond milk, and chia seeds. This smoothie will fill you without raising your blood sugar levels since it is packed with fiber, protein, and healthy fats.

Ingredients:

- 1 cup of mixed berries (such as strawberries, blueberries, and raspberries)
- A single cup of unsweetened almond milk

- One-third cup of chia seeds

Steps:

1. Fill a blender with 1 cup of mixed berries. Depending on what you have available, use fresh or frozen berries.
2. The blender should be filled with 1 cup of unsweetened almond milk.
3. The blender should be filled with 1 spoonful of chia seeds.
4. The smoothie is complete and smooth when the ingredients are mixed at high speed for 30 to 60 seconds.
5. In case more honey, stevia, or maple syrup is required, taste the smoothie and adjust the sweetness to your liking.
6. To enjoy it right away, pour the smoothie into a glass.

Optional Additions:
- One serving of protein powder for added protein
- 1 tablespoon of peanut or almond butter as an additional source of healthy fats
- Add half a banana for more sweetness and creaminess.
- For more fiber and minerals, grab a handful of spinach or kale.

Avocado Slices Seasoned With Sea Salt

An effortless and wholesome snack to make is sliced avocado with sea salt. Sea salt adds a flavorful kick and vital electrolytes, while avocado is a powerhouse of potassium, fiber, and heart-healthy fats.

Ingredients:
- Sea salt
- One ripe avocado

Instructions:

1. Remove the pit from the avocado by cutting it in half lengthwise.
2. Slice the avocado flesh into bite-sized pieces after removing the avocado flesh from both sides with a spoon.
3. In a dish or on a plate, arrange the avocado slices.
4. Give the avocado slices a little sea salt sprinkling.
5. Enjoy after serving!

Note: In addition to sea salt, you could also add a squeeze of lime juice or a dusting of chili flakes to the sliced avocado to give it more flavor.

Cauliflower Florets And Hummus

Healthy and filling at any time of the day, broccoli florets and hummus are delicious snacks. The vitamins and minerals in broccoli are excellent, while the protein and good fats in hummus are abundant. They combine to create a filling and delectable snack that will keep you satisfied and energized.

Ingredients:
- Hummus recipe with broccoli florets

Instructions:

1. Under cold water, thoroughly wash the broccoli florets, and then pat them dry with a paper towel.

2. Set the oven's temperature to 400 °F (205 °C).

3. Put parchment paper on a baking pan.

4. The baking sheet should have the broccoli florets laid out in a single layer.

5. Bake for 15 to 20 minutes, or until the broccoli is cooked through and slightly browned.

6. The broccoli should cool for a few minutes after the baking sheet is taken out of the oven.

7. Place the broccoli in a serving bowl.

8. Place a small dish of hummus next to some broccoli after dividing the hummus.

9. Enjoy the hummus after dipping the broccoli florets in it!

Note: Broccoli florets may also be steamed for 5-7 minutes to achieve tenderness without compromising firmness. As a result, their nutrients will be preserved and they will become more bright.

Edamame With Soy Sauce, Garlic, And Steam

A tasty and nutritious snack that is ideal for any time of day is steamed edamame with garlic and soy sauce. Protein, fiber, and other vital components are abundant in edamame, a kind of soybean. It makes for a tasty, satiating, and low-calorie snack when steamed and seasoned with soy sauce and garlic. To cook steamed edamame with garlic and soy sauce, use the instructions provided here.

Ingredients:

- 100 grams of edamame
- Garlic, minced from 2 cloves
- 2 tablespoons of soy sauce
- A tablespoon of sesame oil (optional)

Instructions:

1. Edamame should be well drained after being rinsed in cold water.

2. Water is heated on high until it boils.

3. When the water in the pot becomes boiling, add the edamame and simmer it for 3 to 5 minutes, or until it is soft.

4. The edamame should be rinsed under cold water after being drained in a colander to help it cool down.

5. Sesame oil can be added to a skillet that is already heated over medium heat.

6. When the garlic is aromatic, add the minced garlic to the pan and cook for about 30 seconds.

7. Sesame oil and garlic should be added to the pan along with the edamame.

8. Edamame should be well covered after being added to the skillet with soy sauce.

9. Let the edamame cool for a few minutes after taking the pan from the heat.

10. With garlic and soy sauce, serve the steamed edamame right away.

Whole Wheat Pita Bread And Roasted Eggplant Dip

The roasted eggplant dip often referred to as baba ganoush, is a delectable and nutritious dip that is ideal for a snack or an appetizer. Tahini, lemon juice, and garlic are blended with roasted eggplant to make a creamy and savory dip after the eggplants have been blended until they are soft and supple. Serve with whole wheat pita bread or your preferred veggies for a delectable and wholesome snack.

Ingredients:
- 1 substantial eggplant
- 1/four cup tahini
- Garlic, minced from two cloves
- 2 tablespoons of lemon juice
- Olive oil and 1/2 tsp salt
- Serving slices of whole wheat pita bread

Step-by-Step Instructions:

1. Your oven should be preheated at 375°F (190°C).

2. Wash and dry the eggplant. Use a fork to make numerous holes in the eggplant, and then spread 1 tablespoon of olive oil over the entire thing.

3. For 35 to 45 minutes, or until the skin is browned and the eggplant is soft and tender, roast the eggplant on a baking sheet in the preheated oven.

4. In the meantime, take the eggplant out of the oven and let it cool. The eggplant should be cut in half, and the flesh should be removed with a spoon after it is cold enough to handle.

5. Along with the tahini, garlic, lemon juice, salt, and final tablespoon of olive oil, place the eggplant flesh in a food processor or blender.

6. Using additional olive oil as needed to obtain a smooth consistency, blend the mixture until it is creamy and smooth.

7. Once the dip has been transferred to a serving bowl, top it with a few dabs of extra virgin olive oil and, if preferred, a few pieces of minced parsley.

8. Provide your favorite dipping veggies or whole wheat pita bread alongside the roasted eggplant dip. Enjoy!

Cinnamon And Almond Butter-Topped Baked Apple Slices

An excellent and healthful snack that will sate your sweet desire without packing on the calories is baked apple slices with cinnamon and almond butter. Every time of day may be used to enjoy this dish since it is the ideal balance of sweetness, nuttiness, and spiciness.

Ingredients:
- 2 apples of moderate size
- 2 teaspoons of almond butter
- 1 tsp. of cinnamon

Instructions:

1. Set the oven to 350 F (175 C).

2. Apples should be sliced thinly, to a thickness of 1/4 inch.

3. On a baking sheet with parchment paper already on it, arrange the apple slices.

4. A small bowl should be used to thoroughly combine the almond butter and cinnamon.

5. Spread a thin layer of the almond butter mixture onto each slice of apple using a spoon.

6. Bake the baking sheet for 10 to 12 minutes, or until the apple slices are tender and gently golden.

7. Let the apple slices cool for a few minutes before serving after removing the baking sheet from the oven.

8. In a serving dish, arrange the apple slices and, if preferred, top with more cinnamon.

9. Enjoy while warm.

Note: Any apple variety will work in this recipe, but Honeycrisp or Gala work best because of their sweetness. In order to change up the recipe, try experimenting with various nut butter, such as peanut or cashew.

Low-GI Granola Bars With Seeds And Nuts

For those seeking a balanced and nutritious snack, low-GI granola bars with nuts and seeds make the ideal treat. Making them is simple, and you can make them however you like. Using a combination of nuts, seeds, and oats, we'll make a tasty and healthy snack that's high in fiber and low in sugar for you to enjoy.

Ingredients:
- One cup of rolled oats
- 50 g of uncooked almonds
- Raw cashews in a half-cup
- Chia seeds, 1/4 cup
- 1/4 cup of pumpkin seeds
- 25% of a cup of sunflower seeds
- 1 tablespoon each of coconut oil and honey
- 1 teaspoon vanilla extract, 1/4 teaspoon sea salt

Instructions:

1. Set the oven to 350 F (175 C). Placing parchment paper over a baking dish will help prevent messes.
2. Combine the chia seeds, sunflower seeds, pumpkin seeds, almonds, and rolled oats in a sizable mixing bowl. Blend well.
3. Coconut oil and honey are heated over medium heat in a small saucepan. The mixture should be thoroughly combined and smooth after stirring.
4. Sea salt and vanilla extract are added after removing the honey and coconut oil mixture from the heat.

5. Over the mixture of nuts, oats, and honey, drizzle the mixture of honey and coconut oil. Mix everything together thoroughly by stirring with a spoon.
6. By using your hands or a spatula, firmly press the mixture into the baking dish after pouring it in.
7. Until the granola bars are golden brown on top, bake in the oven for 20 to 25 minutes.
8. Take the baking dish out of the oven and let it cool for at least 10 minutes.
9. Take the granola out of the dish once it has cooled, then slice it into bars in the size you prefer.
10. Your homemade low-GI granola bars are delicious when paired with nuts and seeds.
11. For up to a week, you can keep these bars sealed up in a container. They make a delicious mid-afternoon snack and are perfect to take with you to school or work.

Lentil- And Brown-Rice Soup With Vegetables

A filling and wholesome meal that is quick to prepare and rich in nutrients is vegetable soup with lentils and brown rice. You can use any vegetables you have on hand to make this soup your own, making it ideal for cold days. While vegetables add vitamins and minerals, lentils and brown rice contribute protein and fiber.

Ingredients:

- One tablespoon of olive oil
- 3 cloves of garlic, minced,
- 1 chopped onion
- Four cups of vegetable stock
- Diced tomatoes in one can
- A cup of lentils
- Brown rice, half a cup, uncooked
- Chopped celery
- Two carrots
- Two stalks
- One zucchini
- One teaspoon of dried thyme
- Salt and pepper.

Instructions:

1. Medium-high heat is used to warm the olive oil in a big pot. For 3 to 5 minutes, until they are translucent, add the onion and garlic.
2. Lentils, brown rice, carrots, celery, zucchini, thyme, salt, and pepper should all be added to the pot along with the vegetable broth. All ingredients should be mixed together.

3. When the rice and lentils are cooked, about 30 to 40 minutes after bringing the soup to a boil, turn the heat down to a simmer.

4. The pot should be taken off the heat so that it can cool.

5. Blend the soup using an immersion blender or in a blender after transferring it.

Advice On How To Maintain a Low-GI Diet While Dining Out And Having Fun With Friends

When eating out and spending time with friends and family, it can be difficult to keep a low-glycemic index (GI) diet. A low-GI diet focuses on consuming foods that release glucose into the bloodstream slowly, resulting in stable blood sugar levels and sustained energy throughout the day.

The GI measures how quickly foods are broken down into glucose and enter the bloodstream. It can be challenging to follow the diet plan, however, because few restaurants and social settings provide options for low-GI meals. In order to maintain a low-GI diet, consider the following suggestions for eating out and socializing:

1) Be prepared: Before going out to eat or to a social event, look up the menu online or give the restaurant a call to inquire about low-GI options. This will enable you to make an informed choice rather than

one that might not be in line with your diet plan when it is made in the heat of the moment.

2) The GI of whole, unprocessed foods is typically lower than that of processed foods, so choose them instead. When eating out, look for dishes with whole grains, lean proteins, and fresh produce.

3) Exercise caution when consuming portions; even low-GI foods can raise blood sugar levels if consumed in large amounts. Regarding portion control, think about splitting an entree or taking leftovers home.

4) White bread, pasta, and sugary drinks are examples of foods with a high GI that should be avoided or consumed in moderation. Find low-GI substitutes like whole grain bread, brown rice, water, and unsweetened tea.

5) Pick healthy fats: Because fats can slow down the absorption of glucose into the bloodstream, it's important to pick healthy fats like olive oil, avocado, and nuts. Trans and saturated fat-rich foods should be avoided.

6) Prevent overeating by staying hydrated. Water can help control blood sugar levels. A spike in blood sugar can be avoided by avoiding sugary beverages.

7) Take the time to savor your meal and pay attention to your body's cues that it is getting hungry and full. When using electronics or talking on the phone while eating, be careful.

8) Be sociable and energetic: Rather than just eating, concentrate on interacting with people and doing things. You can do this to maintain your activity level and dietary awareness.

9) Be adaptable: Keep in mind that following a low-GI diet is not always possible in all circumstances. Keep the overall diet plan in mind, but be flexible and allow yourself the occasional indulgence.

It is possible to maintain a low-GI diet while dining out and having social interactions with friends and family by using these suggestions. You can live a healthy, balanced lifestyle and still partake in social activities with some preparation and thoughtful decision-making.

Chapter 6: Glycemic Index Management for Diabetes and Other Health Conditions

Diabetes Management Using The Glycemic Index

How rapidly foods with carbs boost blood sugar levels is determined by the glycemic index (GI). Based on how a food affects blood sugar levels, this approach assigns a number to each food. Blood sugar control for those with diabetes is essential, and using the GI can help with this task.

An individual with diabetes' body will produce more insulin in response to consuming a high-GI diet in order to assist in controlling blood sugar levels. Consuming meals with a high GI on a regular basis over time may result in insulin resistance, which may eventually lead to type 2 diabetes. In addition, blood vessels and nerves can be harmed by high blood sugar, which can result in life-threatening problems including heart disease, renal failure, and blindness.

People with diabetes can improve the effectiveness of their blood sugar management by including low-GI items in their diet. Due to the slower rate at which these meals are metabolized, blood sugar levels gradually rise over time. By enhancing the body's ability to create insulin, issues like insulin resistance are less likely to occur.

Low-GI foods include things like non-starchy veggies, whole grains, legumes, nuts, and low-sugar fruits like berries. As a result of these meals' typically high fiber content, the digestion, and absorption of carbs are slowed down.

The GI is only one component to take into account while controlling diabetes, it is vital to remember that. Other crucial factors include the amount of food consumed, the total amount of carbohydrates, and individual variations in metabolism. Diabetes sufferers can develop a tailored meal plan that takes these considerations into account by speaking with a qualified dietitian or another healthcare practitioner.

Is a low-GI diet beneficial for other medical issues as well?
Those with diabetes and those who have other medical issues alike can benefit from a low-GI diet. A low-GI diet may be beneficial for the following health conditions:

1. The hormonal condition known as PCOS, which affects women, is called polycystic ovary syndrome. Polycystic ovaries, excessive hair growth, and

irregular periods are its defining traits. Insulin resistance, which can result in type 2 diabetes, is also a danger for PCOS-afflicted women. An eating plan low in glycemic index (GI) can help treat PCOS symptoms by lowering insulin resistance and regulating blood sugar levels.

2. Cardiovascular disease: Studies have indicated that a low-GI diet can lower blood pressure, improve blood cholesterol levels, and reduce inflammation. The risk of cardiovascular disease, one of the main causes of mortality globally, can be decreased by taking into account each of these variables.

3. Obesity: By lowering appetite and fostering feelings of fullness, a low-GI diet can aid in weight management. As a result, calorie consumption may be decreased, assisting in weight loss. Moreover, a low-GI diet has been demonstrated to enhance insulin sensitivity, which can aid in delaying the onset of type 2 diabetes.

4. Type 2 diabetes and cardiovascular disease are more likely to develop in people who have metabolic syndrome, a collection of diseases. These ailments consist of abnormal cholesterol levels, high blood pressure, excessive blood sugar, and extra belly fat. A low-GI diet can lower the risk of metabolic

syndrome by enhancing blood sugar regulation and lowering inflammation.

5. Constipation: A low-GI diet may be beneficial for some constipation conditions, such as irritable bowel syndrome (IBS). The symptoms of bloating, gas, and stomach discomfort might be lessened and bowel movements can be more regularly regulated with a low-GI diet.

Guidelines For Collaborating With a Healthcare Provider To Include Low-GI Eating In Your Treatment Plan

Working with a healthcare provider to include this eating strategy in your treatment plan is crucial if you have a medical condition that might benefit from a low-glycemic index (GI) diet. Here are some pointers for collaborating with your healthcare provider:

1) Seek a medical expert who is educated about the glycemic index and how to control blood sugar levels.

2) Discuss your eating habits and any difficulties you may have to implement a low-GI eating plan with your healthcare provider in a direct and honest manner.

3) Ask for specific suggestions for low-GI foods and meal-planning methods that suit your preferences and way of living.

4) Establish reasonable objectives and monitor your development with the assistance of your healthcare provider. Appreciate your accomplishments and, if necessary, make changes.

5) If you want individualized nutrition guidance and assistance, think about working with a licensed dietitian.

6) Have low-GI items on hand at home and at work to prepare meals and snacks in advance.

7) To find hidden sources of nutrients with a high glycemic index (GI), such as added sugars and processed carbs, carefully read product labels.

8) To make low-GI eating more pleasurable and enduring, experiment with different dishes and cooking methods.

9) Joining an online forum or support group that focuses on low-GI diet and diabetes control will help you stay interested and motivated.

10) While a low-GI diet is just one part of treating diabetes, keep it in mind. Make careful to go by the recommendations of your medical expert on your medicine, exercise program, and other treatment-related decisions.

Conclusion

In summary, implementing the Glycemic Index Food Guide Chart into your diet can be a helpful strategy for promoting healthy eating and controlling certain medical issues. Your blood sugar levels can be stabilized and your chance of developing chronic illnesses is decreased by selecting low-GI meals.

It's critical to keep in mind that the Glycemic Index should be used in conjunction with other dietary advice from a healthcare provider because it's only one component of a balanced diet.

Several resources are available if you're interested in adopting a low-GI diet as part of your way of life. Aside from thinking about taking culinary lessons or nutrition seminars, look for cookbooks and recipe websites that concentrate on low-GI meals.

As well as supporting general health and blood sugar control, regular exercise and stress management practices can also be helpful. Never forget to talk to a doctor before making major dietary changes, particularly if you have a health issue.

All things considered, the Glycemic Index Food Guide Chart can be a useful tool for encouraging good eating habits and lowering the risk of chronic illness. You may live a better, more balanced life by being aware of your choices and keeping educated.

Made in the USA
Coppell, TX
26 March 2023

14768146R00154